"This book will be a g̶   ̶sed,
anxious or suffering fr̶   ̶is a
fantastic practitioner w̶   ̶ʳeat
that we can have access   ̶ᵤₙ expertise and
excellence with this book. I will be recommending this book to
my patients in General Practice and also in my Addiction work."

Dr Youssef Beaini. 'GPs: Behind Closed Doors' and The Bonds Clinic for Addiction.

"As a leading practising Consultant Psychiatrist with 45 years experience of treating all aspects of mental health, I would highly recommend the methods of psychotherapy that Catherine outlines in her book".

Dr Amal Y Beaini, MB, BCH, MRCPsych, FRCPsych, Consultant Psychiatrist, Honorary Senior Lecturer in Psychiatry, Leeds University.

Acknowledgements

First I would like to dedicate this book to LIFE itself and its ability to perform a transformation from darkness into light. When we have the ability to see, sense and feel all that life brings to us and embrace it with acceptance and without fear it can change us into the best version of ourselves

Life has taught me that both good and bad experiences provide us with all we require.

Yesterday I
was clever,
so I wanted
to change
the world.

Today I am
wise, so I
am changing
myself.

-Rumi

My Mum and Dad who are sadly no longer with us, but, without I would not be here. Due to their very different characteristics and personalities which were very starkly different I carved out my own character and eventually found balance.

Thank you to Scott and Darren my sons whom at some low times were my passion and reason for living (that's love at work). You both display different aspects of personality and character to each other too and have taught me in your different ways THE

4

POWER OF UNCONDITIONAL LOVE, so thank you both.

I guess life and its up's and down's will have carved and shaped you both and will continue to do so. I hope that you can and will EXPRESS not REPRESS your feelings. I am here to listen whilst ever I am in this life, but that won't mean me being the expert and asking you to conform to my ideas. For to be free you will formulate your own ideas and feelings. My wish for you is HAPPINESS.

I would also like to say thank you to my patients who have shared so many of their vulnerable and heartfelt stories and trusted in me, it has helped to convince me that this book about expressing feeling and forgiveness to achieve freedom is the way forward for healthy change and growth.

Thanks to the many professionals who have shared the care of these people and one in particular, Dr. Amal Beaini FRCPsych Consultant Psychiatrist who has provided me with knowledge that has enhanced my work and further convinced me that the integration of mind/body medicine in mental health particularly is powerful. He describes this as "The Bio-Psycho-Social Model"

My husband of 25 years to date and wider family and friends and who have encouraged me to write.

To Cheryl Rickman my book coach whose skill and patience has helped me shape and flesh it out when it started as a brain dump. Thank you and now a manifestation of the book!

Adversity truly can be your greatest teacher if we have the resilience to love ourselves and shine bright out of the darkness.

Contents

Life or Lie

By Catherine Taylor MSc Int.Psych

Introduction

This is a book about turning your life around and replacing your fear with forgiveness and freedom.

So who am I to write this book? Well, I'm an ordinary human being who has, by grace, been given 64 years of life thus far, and I pray I will be granted more. I am also a human being who has struggled to understand life or rather MYSELF. I have repressed myself and lied to myself without knowing it, until I managed to dare to EXPRESS myself and turn my unknown LIE into a LIFE.

You will see that as a child, I thought I had been lied to and you will see how, in the end I saw with 20/20 vision that the lies appeared as such, because I was seeing life through convoluted spectacles.

Another reason I feel qualified to write this book is that I've been a practitioner of psychotherapy and mind body medicine for over 20 years, having qualified in Reflexology, Hypnotherapy and gaining a Masters Degree in Psychotherapy many years ago.

My own journey from LIE to LIFE mirrors so many of my clients difficulties. The LIE I speak of is a "false-self made up of false-beliefs", and I will explain where this predicament that we are unaware of comes from. It doesn't come from intentional lies, but from a trans-generational cover up to avoid deep feelings such as blame, shame, failure and rejection.

A theory of lifting you from repression (and depression) to expression (joy and freedom); from living a LIE to living a good LIFE is outlined in this book.

The Mental Health Taboo

Some might say that depression in human beings is normal? It's certainly not abnormal. In my experience, it's as common as the common cold. The difference is that the common cold is something people are very comfortable discussing and, in some cases go into competition about whose cold was worse. Whereas, with depression and anxiety, people are not so keen to even admit they have suffered at all.

Sadly, even in 2019 mental health can still be taboo. The stigma around mental health and illness is gradually lifting. But there is so much work to be done. An interesting fact I have gleaned from clients, is there seems to be a feeling that anxiety is more accepted than depression. In fact clients have often wanted to make sure I was aware they were anxious and NOT DEPRESSED.

Trans-generationally and socially, people are afraid to admit that they feel down and anxious, or tell someone that they have obsessional compulsive disorders. Interestingly though it is still ok to divulge that we have appendicitis, arthritis, diabetes, high blood pressure, broken a limb or worse still, had a diagnosis of cancer or other life-threatening illness.

The reactions to these physical illnesses are absolutely different to saying, "I am depressed." If you have a physical ailment, people respond with empathy and concern. Often a word of hope and get well wishes are sent, along with flowers and offers of help. Sadly, if you say you are depressed then it is usually met with a comment of "oh, you'll be ok", or worse, "pull yourself together". No get well card. No offer of help.

So depressed or anxious people hide their illness and put on a smile. The response to that is "oh, but you look fine!" Contrary to the physical ailment met with "you look pale, are you getting enough rest, please don't overdo it". Sufficient is this lack of concern and compassion for mental illness that a lot of my patients have reported to me that they'd prefer to have a physical illness, not for the sympathy, but so they could get a treatment plan and a time for recovery.

The hope provided with a six or twelve week recovery plan where, by the end of treatment you'd be back to normal, would help so much. But there isn't that luxury with depression.

People ask, "how many sessions will it take for me to be well?" Yet, there is no answer. So much is up to them. It all feels like an expedition too big, so patients are frightened as we start to look down the therapeutic microscope. Indeed, the foundation of their pain could be so toxic and corroded that they fear they could be destroyed, never to be put back together again. Like Humpty Dumpty.

Releasing (not removing) the pain

I have to explain at this juncture the good news is that, whatever the foundations of pain are, they haven't been destroyed by that pain, and if the pain hasn't destroyed them by now, it won't. Furthermore they still have the broken pieces. It is absolutely possible to put them back together again.

With physical health we often remove a piece. With depression, the excavation of repressed pain will set them free and the repressed baggage is the very thing that is causing the depression. Expression of that baggage is the very thing that will set them free. We're not removing the pain, we're releasing it through expression, so it fades and is replaced with hope.

This can still be difficult for the patient to hear. It feels like we are doing psychic surgery without any anaesthetic. Because you can't hand them over to the surgeon, you have to be wide awake to the discomfort. Yet they've been anaesthetising their pain for so long, it's what has caused the depression in the first place.

The truth is, even though you have put the pain to the 'back of your mind' it is still there.

While anti-depressants can be very helpful and some people have brain chemistry which benefits well from this intervention, they only serve to numb the pain. They can't remove it. As such, they can be useful painkillers but the problem is still there, so we need something in addition to anti-depressants.

The combination of psychotherapy, self-inquiry and medication is far more powerful. And, hopefully, when full expression has taken place the medication may no longer be needed.

Dr AY Beaini FRCPsych Consultant Psychiatrist says "the bio psycho social model plus complementary therapies is the basis for diagnosis and treatment plan in medicine, particularly in mental health". Of course, some people who have organic or chemical imbalance may always need medication, but everyone benefits from being their true selves.

Sadly, Anxiety /Depression/OCD/Neurosis are all as common as a cold, but still the bad cold is more freely expressed and more people are able to join in the conversation and compare symptoms than they are to express their anxiety or other mental issue.

This is a really sad fact as I have a belief in Mind/Body medicine I do believe that stomach ulcers, irritable bowel syndrome and other psychosomatic illnesses originate from the stress response. Thank goodness some of the very influential people in our world are making it part of their plight to bring out attention to depression. People like Prince Harry, Prince William and The Duchess of Cambridge are helping to relieve the shame which is the biggest reason why people try to go it alone in their despair. It's about time because, it is estimated that one in six people will experience a common mental health problem every week.

I have had the privilege of spending thousands of hours with people who have reiterated to me the shame that they feel in not being able to 'pull themselves together.' The Buddha's quote is so potent when he says "do not tell people to pull themselves together, help them through it."

What I hope to achieve in writing this book is to provide a guide for lifting depression and relieving anxiety and, in doing so, helping you through it.

Relief = Re-Life

My formula is that all that we have REPRESSED becomes DEPRESSED and that EXPRESSION is its RELIEF.

I am advocating therefore that pushing pain to the back of your mind (repression) is robbing you of your life and that, as a result of fear, assumptions and trans-generational conditioning, you may be living a lie instead of a life.

To put the F back in the word lie would give you your life back.

What's the F?

I believe, primarily, the 'F' in 'LIFE' is FEELING.

When you don't allow your true feelings, your repressed feelings cause depression and anxiety. And yet, when we remove the shame and the anaesthetic, we can view anxiety and depression differently. We can see them as a warning signal and friendly guide, inviting you to FEEL your way back to life.

I truly believe, if a person can find out who they are and what they want and feel confident enough to express that, without the fear of being rejected, judged or unloved, then depression, anxiety, OCD, frustration can all be minimised. So we need to replace FEARFUL thoughts and lean into FEELING. We'll explore precisely how to do this in the pages of this book.

From love to hate, from jealousy and pride to guilt and confusion, from sadness and anger to frustration - we repress so many feelings, all of which are fear-based.

Equally, there are millions of different stories in a person's life, from cradle to grave, but those millions of stories can only evoke these feelings over and over again. And until they can be felt and dealt with, repression of them can cause depression and a stagnation of life itself.

Expression of them has the power to bring freedom and release from a prison which has been born out of trans-generational programming.

This programming was originally developed to avoid blame, shame and the rejection of not fitting in. We are wired to feel this way, originating from the need to belong to a tribe. Yet, this evolutionary biological design of programming to avoid blame, shame and rejection is actually causing it. The physiological and psychological fear of rejection today is as powerful as it was thousands of years ago when rejection from a tribe meant you wouldn't survive alone. And yet, we can survive nowadays. We can rebuild our lives and grow, whatever pain we have endured.

Yet, wanting to go our own way is still sometimes a very frightening journey if others do not approve. Sometimes not agreeing with our families or partners way of doing things can make us feel that we are in danger, if we express it, for fear of that painful rejection. The mind in trying to avoid that rejection tries to convince us that the idea we don't agree with is not so bad after all. In truth the mind is finding a way to avoid what it believes the heart is going to suffer: that painful rejection. This is a battle then between the head and the heart. The heart is the one that says I really could be excited about my idea and the head says "well I wouldn't if I were you unless you want to be lonely, because they won't agree". That's when the mind starts to find a type of 'attic' where the real self is stored and then you carry on with the false self, 'the please others self' then start to live the lie and not the life.

In healing myself and creating this book, I hope to heal others, like you. In this way, I can use my own story to heal others, a co-destiny that my mum, dad and I, all share. (See my own story in Chapter 1) my dad was right - something good can come from something bad!

I hope this book will help you to remember or rather re-member yourself. To find all the split-off parts of you and piece the true you back together again.

I hope it will help you to find the courage to allow yourself to be responsible and loyal to yourself; to learn to express yourself without been afraid of losing or being rejected.

I know, from countless experiences with my own patients that the outcome from expressing feelings rather than repressing them is joy and freedom. I've also discovered the knock on effect is wonderful news. Often, when they've started to un-repress themselves and express their true self, clients report their family is more respectful of them and seem more interested in them. I jokingly ask if they've been going to therapy as well, but they haven't. So I ask my client, "Are you respecting yourself more? Are you more interested in you?" "Oh definitely I am," they reply.

It seems that life is truly a mirror and it reflects back to us what we think of ourselves. If we have repressed all our bright and happy thoughts at the back of our minds, then that is how life seems to reflect dull and hidden. But, when we bring our bright and joyful self out into expression, it seems to reflect back bright and happy.

> My wish for you in this book is that your life
> becomes a bright and joyful reflection, so that you
> can enjoy your journey, your journey called LIFE.

Don't tell
someone to
get over it.
Help them
get through it.

CHAPTER 1
Our interwoven stories

The way we are wired

Us humans - we aim to please. It's an evolutionary tendency which has stayed with us since we lived in tribes. Impressing the rest of our tribe was vital in order to stay in it. Being admired and valued was a matter of survival. It's why we care so much about what others think of us today, even though now it's more about social relevance than survival. These days our family is our first tribe and wanting to please them remains important.

But this need to please can stunt our growth and keep us stuck. People pleasing is at our own expense.

This, and a great many other incidents which happen to us as we grow from the freedom we experience at birth to the prisons we find ourselves in, can cause us to lose ourselves and lose our mental health.

That's why I've written this book: because of my own journey and the common patterns I've noticed between my own and the journeys of my clients, to guide you from repression to expression, from trapped in your past to freedom for your future.

I've lived with both anxiety and depression myself and know how it feels to live both in a dark fog and in a whirlwind of despair. I've spent thousands of hours with others who have felt like that too. I've come out the other side and, over the past 20 years as a Psychotherapist, I've helped many others to do so too.

My clients have tried to fix themselves in many ways. And when they've not been able to fix whatever they believe is wrong with them, they self-soothe.

Attempts at self-soothing range from over-eating - leading to feelings of disgust and self-hatred and over-drinking - leading to alcoholism and all manner of problems, to shop-a-holic behaviour and gambling. All attempts to self-soothe, which may feel better temporarily, but in the long run don't work and, in most cases make things far worse.

Some people self-soothe, others simply live with feeling like there's something wrong with them, often caused by rejection or another trauma in their lives.

We all have back stories relating to what lies beneath our mental health issues.

My story - "is the world a lie?"

I was an only child born in 1955 to loving parents. I found out much later that my mum had miscarried six babies, until I came along.

You'd have thought this might have made me feel extra special. However, the converse is true. Despite my mum telling me how much I was wanted, I often felt unwanted and a nuisance.

During the school holidays, when I was four years old, my mum and dad sent me to the seaside with my grandma, aunties and cousins. My cousins were having a fabulous time, but I felt afraid, lonely and quite miserable. I just wanted my mum. I just wanted to go home.

In the middle of the holiday, my mum and dad arrived by bus as we didn't have a car. They had come to join us at the seaside for my 5th Birthday.

"Happy Birthday Catherine" I heard my mum say, "do you love me?" I replied. "Yes," she said. "So can I come home with you please? I don't like it here". "I will ask the bus driver," she replied. I thought to myself, 'what has the bus driver got to do with my mum loving me?'

Of course, it never occurred to me about how it might be to do with paying the fare or to find out whether there was a seat on the bus.

"Is the world a lie" I asked her. "I don't know what you mean Catherine," she replied.

I thought to myself, "well, it must be a lie, because you said you love me, you know I'm not happy and now you're asking the bus driver if I can come home?! My secret thoughts were, "really I'm a nuisance and you're not saying it out loud."

How early assumptions can be made. How early incongruence can be felt. And how early these thinking traps kick off a whole thought process of inaccurate storytelling and damaging beliefs.

From that moment on I thought I was adopted because, for a lady who desperately wanted a child I didn't feel wanted.

I can remember her showing me a photograph of me as a baby. I was a pretty fat baby. The photo showed my mum looking worn out and thin. "Look at you and look at me," she said. "You sucked the life out of me!"

I now know she was proud that she had me well fed, which, in those days was proof of a good mother, yet I took it literally and inaccurately thought I had nearly killed my mother! Children take things literally and, it wasn't until I talked about this in my own therapy, that I was able to think about it more deeply.

As a mother myself I cringe at what I may have said to my own children, without realising the impact. And yet, we can only do our best and should not feel guilty.

Another occasion, I fell off a swing and cut my head open. My friend said, "Let's go to your mum." Knowing that my mother was a nervous and anxious lady, I begged my friend to let me go to her mum instead. "No" replied my friend, "your mum will help". In the end, I did go to my mum and, instead of empathy, I got a good telling off for falling off and a smack because this incident was going to make her late for work. My friend ran off and couldn't believe my mum hadn't given me love and empathy like her mum would have. So, again, I just thought I was a nuisance, making mum unhappy.

I think that's when I began to numb my feelings. It was quite overwhelming to feel that I was a problem to her and making her unhappy or angry.

Another time, we had gone on holiday with an aunty and uncle who didn't have children. The weather was bad. The seaside in England usually wasn't the best. They passed a pub and I heard them say, "If we didn't have Catherine with us, we could go in there". 'Oh, they would be better off without me,' I thought. In the 1960s, children weren't allowed in pubs and children who had brothers and sisters could sometimes sit in the car with pop and crisps whilst the parents were in the pub.

I now know they didn't mean what I heard and they were probably not wishing to prevent my aunty and uncle from going in the pub. Yet my early thoughts and interpretation still brought about a lonely and isolated feeling.

Of course my parents knew nothing of this and I would try harder to smile and look happy and please them and not bring anxiety upon them, because I didn't want to be the cause of their spoilt enjoyment, I just desired to feel loved and wanted.

Now, through a lot of work on myself, I can see that I was wanted and loved, but I now understand it was almost impossible for my mum to feel that and show it. What a shame that I'd spent all of my childhood and a big part of my adult life not knowing that my mum couldn't demonstrate love for me and concluding she maybe didn't want me - a false, inaccurate thought, which I repeated so often it became a belief and formed my own mental schema and led to my lack of self worth, anxiety and depression.

Mum

I know my mum was a hurt and anxious person.

She was the eldest of seven children. My youngest aunty was only 11 years older than me, so mum had taken on a lot of responsibility helping to raise her siblings. She lost her fiancée in the war and then, if that wasn't heart breaking enough, she had lost six babies.

"Of course" I thought. How could a lady who had so much loss attach to anybody? To her, attachment meant potential loss! So, to survive, to protect herself from further heartbreak, she had to anaesthetise her feelings.

Poor lady. And all those years I'd inaccurately believed it was all about me. But no, it was about her. From the age of five, I'd assumed she didn't want or love me but how could she show her feelings? Doing so would put her at risk of feeling more pain, so she repressed them.

Trans-generationally, two lives had been adversely affected from repression. She's missed out on having a loving relationship with the one child who did survive and I had spent my entire life believing a false-belief. And, as a result, I became a people pleaser.

Back in those days they didn't offer therapy to people who had lost babies or loved ones in the war. There was no time to feel feelings. You were expected to "Keep Calm and Carry On". And so you did.

Bless my dear mum, she was a hurt person. She was courageous too. She had so many surgeries in her life. The last surgery could have left her paralysed but she was so brave.

When she was young she got a bad fever and had to go to an outdoor school for a while to recover. I think, when she was ill, it was the most attention she ever got. Now I am not saying she was ill to get attention but, in the end, she seemed scared to live and scared to die.

She was a beautiful writer with her right hand, but did everything else left-handed. She had been brought up a Catholic and the nuns had hit her with the cane for being left-handed and had called her 'the Devil's child'. No wonder she had been hardened. She had some big feelings to repress. What a message for a child to be given. Hurt people, hurt people.

The Catholic priest had told her she could not marry my dad because he was a member of the Church of Scotland . My mum told the priest "well God made him and, if he is good enough for God then he is good enough for me". That was a courageous thing to do in the 1940s. My dad said he would change to be a Catholic and my mum said no. She'd rather marry a good non-Catholic man than a Catholic who wasn't a good man.

So my mum had courage and fight in her. She was feisty and had a mind of her own. She was hurt too. And maybe, through being hurt, that's what she expected and that's what she got. More pain. As my mum grew older she got Alzheimer's disease and it got worse when she knew my Dad was going to die. I think she had never really had a childhood and had responsibility from too young an age, so she dearly wanted someone to take over. In the end, for the last decade of her life, she needed full time care in a care home.

Throughout her life, she didn't have access to her feelings so just stayed in her own world. There was also an ingrained belief, as a result of the pain she suffered, that the world had something against her, even God.

When I went to tell my mum, who was in hospital with septicaemia at the time, that my dad had died, she shouted to the hospital priest, "I am finished with God he has taken my husband!" Of course, it's no wonder she took it personally, after all the loss she had suffered in her life.

The poor lady couldn't even attach to her own life in the end.

This should not be the case.

If only she'd loved herself. She was a child once and probably thought her only role in life was to be responsible for everything that happened. Only, sadly for her, she didn't know how to be positive and reap her belief that life would work out for her. She was so set in her ways and had repressed her feelings for so long, she was unable to turn the lie into a LIFE.

Dad

Conversely, my dad saw something retrievable and saw that there was always something to be positive about in everything. He was the right man for her and the absolutely perfect dad and grandad for me and my two boys. He brought light amidst the darkness. He was our silver lining and he helped us to see the silver lining too.

My husband and my son's father lost his way to drink. I am not fully sure what his repressed stuff was but he lost the battle. My dad became father to my two boys and how blessed we all were to have him.

As a school child, whenever I said to my parents, 'I can't do this, I may come bottom of the class.' My mum would say 'well somebody has to come bottom'. It makes me laugh now, because that was true and perhaps wise too. I was trying my best, but I only interpreted it as 'my mum doesn't care.'

My dad, however, would say "mind over matter." He'd encourage me to believe that I could do it, rather than think I couldn't. There are so many books now on the positivity of the mind; he had it.

And he showed he cared. He still kept his feelings in and didn't express them often, but he was able to find some kind of balance, as he found the positive in each situation.

He may not have had a wonderful SatNav to guide him, which only comes from introducing feeling to proceedings, but he had a positive mindset, which helped. And that positivity attracted more of what he loved - including two wonderful grandsons for him to help me care for.

Interestingly though, I repressed my own feelings and continued to be a people pleaser throughout my life. I wanted to please my dad, because he had enough on his plate, dealing with mum. I wanted to please my mum, because I was desperate for her to show love to me. I didn't realise that hurt people hurt people, so I continued on this path of people pleasing until I saw how detrimental it was to repress and suppress my feelings.

Finding our way from our way

In her book, *You Can Heal Your Life,* Louise Hay suggests that the parents we have are always the right ones. I believe her. In my own case I learned to change my people pleasing into a better model. 'Empathy for others and empathy for myself'. If I had two parents who were telling me how wonderful I was all the time I could have got the idea I was special and not developed empathy for others. I may not have embarked on training to be a psychotherapist which helped me express my own repression. Evidently, "what is in your way is your way", as long as you work with it and don't repress it, as I found out.

Now I can truly thank what I thought was my adversity. For it has led to live my true path and be my true self. I am stronger because of everything I've been through. I believe I am now more than I thought I could be. I am just sorry that the older generations did not have the opportunity to work through their own adversities - to express rather than repress and suppress - and live a LIFE rather than a LIE.

Over time I was able to release my feelings and set myself free, and all I've been through myself has helped me to help others to set themselves free too. Because, we're in this together.

Indeed, as I've run my own practice, I've noted that I'm not the only one to be a people pleaser.

John's story

John was 30 years old when I met him; married, a father of two. He was running his own Optician's practice. An extremely well groomed and polite man, no one would ever know this man had a problem. In fact, on the contrary, many would think he was a successful and happy man with everything going for him. Everything on the outside looked enviable.

The psychiatrist's letter read as follows: John was experiencing a 'living nightmare, afraid of his own shadow, waking every morning with a feeling of dread and mental torment'.

He presented to me that he was anxious and he "worried about worrying". He had psychosomatic symptoms i.e. panic attacks and irritable bowel syndrome. He often felt dizzy and short of breath. He said he had felt suicidal in the past and been on anti-depressant medication which didn't seem to help at the time.

These symptoms had been investigated by a physician to see if there was anything wrong with his heart (shortness of breath), he had undergone investigations with regard to his digestive system, i.e. bowel, stomach, oesophagus. Blood tests had been taken and even an MRI scan of his brain, to see if there was an obstruction that could be causing the dizziness

Thankfully he was physically well. He had no disease. However John was at DIS-EASE within himself and his symptoms were real. His symptoms FELT real in his body.

At the age of four, John can remember expecting his mum to come and pick him up from nursery. But granddad appeared instead. When he asked, "where's mum?" His granddad answered: "Your mum has gone. She doesn't want you, so you will live with me and grandma". Overwhelmed with feeling unloved and rejected and not wanting (or being able) to take this in, four-year-old John screamed, 'I WANT MY MUM" and his grandad repeated, "WELL SHE DOESN'T WANT YOU!"

As any psychotherapist would know, this would later become a PTSD (Post Traumatic Stress Disorder) and potentially a DID (Dissociative Identity Disorder) where a person experiencing shock feels separate from their body.

As John sat in front of me sharing his story, he revealed that his father had been ill and his mum wasn't enjoying being his father's carer. She didn't seem to have the ability to respond to the responsibility of a sick husband and young child. So instead, she found herself another man who was well, so she could enjoy herself and not have responsibility.

Imagine, being four years old, a small child and, even though you don't have many verbal skills yet, the words "SHE DOESN'T

WANT YOU" rang in his ears and through his thoughts, feelings and emotions. From that moment on you would naturally wonder, 'but why doesn't she?' And then you'd make your own assumptions, write your own story and come to your own, probably inaccurate conclusions, which may involve self-blame, self-loathing and create a strong fear of rejection that would stay with you throughout your life.

He must have wondered, as we are wired with a negativity bias, whether it was something he had done to send his mum away? Grandad never explained to him that she did not have the capacity to love and take care of herself, let alone look after a child. Grandad was probably angry with her and thought explaining to a four year old would be fruitless. What's more, grandad himself was probably taking on the responsibility that was too much for him.

Trans-generationally granddad probably didn't have the skills to process his own feelings and so just got on with the duty of bringing up his grandson, which was sterling. Older generations thought emoting was an interruption to getting on with the task at hand. They had a 'keep calm and carry on' mindset.

But imagine trying to 'keep calm and carry on' when your mother has abandoned you and you are four!

As if this rejection wasn't enough for a small child to deal with, at some level, John also knew that his dad may die (his father had suffered a brain haemorrhage). This will have been like a tsunami to his emotions; too big to manage. But, as he screamed and cried his poor little heart out, granddad told him, "there is no point in doing that." i.e. Don't feel your feelings!

From this moment on, John, without knowing it, started to anaesthetise his emotional pain. It was an intelligent move at the time and probably an automatic physiological reaction. Just as when we are automatically rendered unconscious when we are hit by a car or have a tragic fall. It is a function of the body to shut down until we receive medical help.

From four years old until he was a teenager, John remembers living out this unconscious autopilot in a state of 'numbing compliance' just so he might belong somewhere, just so this terrible ordeal would never happen to him again.

So John began to exist to please others. He'd avoid mentioning his own needs, (if he even knew what they were). When a child is so rejected the mind says "I know how the world works, don't EXPRESS your needs REPRESS them, don't FEEL your FEELINGS, NUMB THEM. People don't love you if you do these things, you just become a nuisance!"

When John became a teenager he was still a 'People Pleaser' but, this time, he used his script to please the wrong crowd so that he might belong and be a part of something. He was an only child and he was determined to have friends now. But to fit in, John began using drugs and shoplifting. He then felt guilty (mad, bad and sad) because he'd let down the man and woman who had stuck by him and loved him, for he was old enough to understand their sacrifice and their loyalty.

Somewhere in his mind, he had wondered and then began to believe that he was a bad boy and, perhaps that was why mum didn't want him. His mind ran through all the what ifs of whether had he been a better or more loveable little boy, she would never have gone away. Even though he was only four and couldn't understand the truth, he created a story in his mind that her absence was somehow his fault.

So now in his teens, even though he knew it was wrong to do so, he was acting out the badness he believed himself to be.

He had never processed the feelings and emotions of sadness, anger and rage that he felt towards his mother after she abandoned him, because it didn't seem appropriate and the adults looking after him had never processed it with him, and he knew he must not for fear of causing other people to abandon him. He felt the shame and the blame that his mother should have owned and he simply anaesthetised the lot to protect himself from further rejection. He buried those feelings deep inside, repressed, and that repression turned into depression.

He had self-harmed frequently by cutting himself, a way people with numbed feelings try to FEEL something. Whilst they are feeling the pain they tell me it feels good, but it doesn't last. John had also tried to commit suicide, although he admits it was a cry for help. The cry was really to his frozen self, which was acting out all his pain and, in turn, serving people to reject him again and again.

Despite all of his repressed heartache, he managed to do well at school and go to university. He became an optician, fell in love and yet he built a wall so the love was surface-driven and he would doubt it at times. When John's depression hit, he thought the love of his life would not want to continue living with a pleaser and someone who wasn't "the life and soul of the party." Depression is often coupled with thoughts of unworthiness.

When John became my client, he admitted that he did not feel his feelings, slowly he began to grasp why his feelings had been numbed. "I don't know how to feel" said John. "Somewhere inside of me I know I could do with a really good cry, but it won't come. Sometimes I feel a lump in my throat as though the sadness is blocked."

And so it was.

Sometimes, those who've numbed their own feelings a long time ago can retrieve feelings through another medium, for example, by listening to the news or watching sad films or songs; perhaps a song which meant something to them at a time when feelings were alive.

For John his feelings had been repressed, numbed and unexpressed for so long, this was a little trickier.

As John watched his children develop, he could see how vulnerable they were and could see how such cruel news being imparted to his own children would evoke sadness and anger. As a result of imagining this hurt he was able to talk about feeling frustrated (which, I believe, is a combination of sadness and anger).

Remember John had expressed anger and sadness in the nursery yard but was told to repress it. And that began to make sense as he feared expressing his feelings would cause annoyance and so he would be rejected again and he would never belong. He decided he'd be safer if he stopped feeling altogether.

He had lived like that from 4 years old until 30 years old when I met him. Not that he hadn't tried to get help before we met. He had tried Cognitive Behavioural Therapy (CBT) but, for him, it was like a plaster on a gaping wound. He had tried to think differently and let things go but the feelings continued to be repressed which locked in the depression.

Anxiety was knocking on the door to set them free and fear was saying "don't feel - it will be the end of you if you feel the tsunami of emotion that's buried deep inside."

By now, John's mum had expressed a wish to be part of her grandchildren's lives.

John was trying to allow that, but it was frustrating him. He was trying to be the bigger person. Of course, understandably he wanted, at times, to tell her where to go - to do unto her what had been done to him. And yet, despite being hurt himself, he had an awareness about hurting others.

Together we worked out that her wish to be part of his family and causing him frustration was a good thing. How so? You may say. It was a good thing because frustration was a feeling, so it was evoking emotions in him that he now had permission to actually FEEL. He was old enough and could pay his own bills and had a wife and children. He had a foundation and permission to 'feel his feelings'. Of course feelings of frustration weren't the most pleasant of feelings but they had come into the recovery room - an important first step toward healing.

Remember, the anaesthetic means if we can't feel the bad, we can't feel the good either. So, as a result of anaesthetising his feelings, he'd disabled his ability to feel good. So, although it may sound perverse to say, it was actually a win for him to try to manage his mum's request and allow himself to feel those old repressed feelings. In doing so he could begin to remove the anaesthetic and begin to feel the good as well as the bad.

He managed to say a few things to her. He explained he was attending therapy and had needed to see a psychiatrist. Interestingly, rather than sympathising or apologising she focused on her own woes, which made him angry. But again, he was beginning to feel.

Eventually, he realised for himself that his mother had no regard for herself. She was in a relationship with someone who also had no regard for himself. He began to see that the treatment of him was not about him, it was about a woman who had no self love, who was bankrupt herself of love. She had no empathy for his suffering because she didn't feel. Life was robotic and people were commodities to her. Once he saw this for himself, admittedly after a long time, he started to feel sorry for this woman. And, when those feelings of empathy began, he started to be able to 'forgive her, for she knew not what she did'. Through this journey of healing, he went from frustration and anger to empathy and, eventually, he got to the best place - forgiveness.

We know that forgiveness doesn't mean you condone what someone has done, but it sets you free from the harsh feelings of anger, bitterness, hate and revenge which are dangerous for the body and mind.

Many spiritual teachers on miraculous healing like Louise Hay say, when full healing hasn't occurred, more forgiveness is needed. We will delve into this in more detail in Chapter 5.

For John, forgiveness set him free and gave him his feelings back. He was able to apply feeling his feelings to his own life and family. Moving from repression to expression reduced a lot of his psychosomatic symptoms and he is now physically and mentally much better.

Today John's SatNav is a more accurate guide.

When John first came to me, as he still had low self-esteem, he was always looking at buying another business. Each time he achieved something it never satisfied him, he was like the proverbial bucket with a hole in it. He was only as good as his last fix. Together we saved him from making some very poor business decisions. Once he began to heal he no longer needed his possessions and achievements to validate him.

The narcissistic wounding of his mother rejecting him had to be fixed every day, otherwise he was depressed and anxious that he was going to be rejected again.

Once his feelings were restored he knew when he did not have a good gut feel. He stopped attracting people who saw him as desperate for a fix and presenting ideas to him that weren't in his best interest. As he started to have more self worth, other people started to respect him. His own self-worth was mirrored back to him. He had less anxiety to prove himself as worthwhile. He started to know he was a success BECAUSE of his story, not DESPITE it

John used his adversity to develop himself into a good husband, father, business man, grandson and son. He used feeling his frustration to heal himself. And he used forgiveness to free himself from the pain. He expressed his suppressed emotions and he let go of the fear that entrapped him.

I remember John before he left therapy speaking with real feeling about his grandparents. He could now see with 20/20 vision from an adult point of view, the love and loyalty they had afforded him. He had soothed his own inner hurt and angry child with the truth after he had worked it all through. So now, he could let go of the old story, for he had obtained a lot of wisdom about life.

And therein lies the key - only when we express our repressed feelings can we begin to move forward. Only then can we let go and grow. No matter what age we are when we first begin to numb our feelings.

Mine and John's stories share the similarities of feeling rejected as children, repressing the feelings relating to that rejection and people-pleasing driven by fear of more rejection. However, people can numb their feelings at any point in life. It isn't always as a result of childhood adversity. It can happen at any age, when a trauma, shock, bad news or grief occurs. I have seen mothers go numb after losing a child or numb their feelings after a relationship break-up or loss of a pet. So while there are a million different stories, there are only so many feelings to be numbed. And in numbing some, we numb them all.

Anaesthetising feelings can be the body's natural defence for a while, just like being unconscious when hit by a bus, so the person can recover. It's when the repression of feeling continues that depression and other issues occur.

Now John had expressed his feelings and found the pearls of wisdom amongst the adversities he'd endured.

He now had the wisdom to pass on to his own children.

He had moved from Fear to Freedom and he knew the formula for putting the F into what had been a LIE to create a good LIFE from then on. He was free.

I spoke to John a few months ago to tell him I was hoping to use his story but change his name. He said he was very happy for that to happen. I asked how he was doing?

"I am very happy," he smiled. "I am kind to myself now. I allow my wife to do things to help and I believe I deserve it. I am not afraid to feel the love from my wife and children."

His own son is a teenager now and he can have open and wise conversations with him and his daughter. His grandparents have passed away and he wrote and spoke a eulogy for his grandfather with feeling.

John still sees his mum.

He says she hasn't changed, but he has.

"The most
important kind of
freedom is to be
who you really are.
You trade in your
reality for a role.

You trade in your
sense for an act.

You give up your
ability to feel and
in exchange
put on a mask"

Jim Morrison

CHAPTER 2
Are you living a LIFE or a LIE?

Born free

When we first enter this world, we are free.

We are free from conditioning, free from opinion and free from messages, stereotypes and suggestions. What's more, we are free to cry and laugh and express ourselves when we are born.

Yet this freedom doesn't last.

Soon we become trapped; estranged from freedom to various extents, depending on our upbringing and to what we're exposed to.

How does this happen? Well, as we journey through our childhood, we become conditioned to believe untruths rather than the freedom of living our own truth.

We get lost. Or rather our true selves become buried underneath all the cultural and parental conditioning, underneath other people's opinions and the consequential inaccurate conclusions that we then assume, underneath the subsequent beliefs about who we are and how we should show up in the world.

It took John 30 years to turn the LIE into a LIFE. To return to the freedom he had before the cause of his repression came about.

But why do we get lost?

We need to belong

It is in part due to our need to belong. Our need to conform, to fit in, to impress is integral to our humanity.

According to Maslow's hierarchy of needs, once our physiological and safety needs are met (food, water, warmth, rest, security and safety) our psychological needs are the next most important. These include belonging and love and they come before our esteem needs and self-fulfilment needs.

We are psychologically wired to want to belong, to prioritise this sense of belonging and of being loved above any other needs such as self-esteem, self-fulfilment or self-actualisation. We are wired to care more about our relationships with other people and about what they think of us, than anything else, other than being fed, warm, rested and safe.

Over time, our beliefs about our actions, behaviour and identity (what we should/shouldn't do, how we should/shouldn't behave and who we should/shouldn't be) are shaped by others - parents, grandparents and other relatives; society, media and peers. And our beliefs become mental schemas about how to live our lives. They literally drive how we show up in the world, who we become and how we respond.

But according to someone else rather than according to our own truth.

External scriptwriters pen our life stories

The power of suggestion is strong and our fear develops at varying levels, depending on the expectations we feel from those bringing us up. So we begin to repress who we are for fear of upsetting others or losing their love or failing to conform to expectations. As such we are cast as characters of our story, rather than the director.

Over the course of the story of our lives, external directors and scriptwriters get in the way of our thriving.

This book aims to help uncover what enables thriving rather than disables it. It will help shine a light on how upbringing brings up barriers to our true selves. And it will uncover how we became estranged from our personal freedom in the first place and what we can do about it?

Have you ever heard of the quote: *"The worst lies we tell are the ones we tell to ourselves"?*

It's quite a quote.

But why would we lie to ourselves?

Generally, once we've been programmed and conditioned into behaviours, we don't even know we are lying to ourselves. Our truth is essentially lost to us. So much so that we can live our entire lives (or most of our lives until we learn how to break free and discover our truth) thinking, assuming and believing mistruths about who we are and why what happens to us happens to us.

Look at John and I - we believed we were essentially unlovable. That became our truth. But it was inaccurate.

As a psychotherapist, I often ask my clients who are depressed, anxious or generally unhappy "who are you?" It's a simple question, yet, interestingly, the answer I usually receive is, "I haven't really thought about it".

Isn't that fascinating?

We think so much about so much else, but not about who we actually are.

As children we are conditioned by other people's ideas, which have been passed down from generation to generation. Often, life-affecting decisions have been made by our ancestors and programmed into their children, who programme them into their children and they programme them into us, and so on and so forth.

And it's not easy to think for ourselves because, we feel disloyal even challenging the conditioning that we now have allegiance to. It's our 'normal', our status quo, so we don't question it. That's how estranged we've become from our own truth.

Hence why, uncovering our conditioned responses is quite an emotional process. When a person first starts to explore their true values, if those values go against all they've been taught, an emotional battle begins.

The person usually starts to investigate who they are and finds a myriad of excuses why it's best to stick to the old way of being. The old way of being seems safer, for it means they needn't risk being rejected by the people in their lives. It brings up a sense of guilt going against the conditioning. Fear strikes of being alone or making a huge mistake that might bring the whole world as they know it crashing down. The risk is too laden with potential misery. It feels like a comfort zone stretch too far.

Setting your true purpose and being free becomes a no-go area in case it brings rejection from what and who you know and from where you believe you belong.

In truth, what sustains misery is to ignore how you truly feel in favour of staying programmed to a way of being that is not really you; to a way of behaving and showing up in the world that is not truly who you are.

So, who are you really?

You are who you believe yourself to be. But therein lies the problem.

Don't believe what you believe

The problem with belief is that it is so frequently inaccurate.

You see, beliefs are formulated when repeated thoughts create neural pathways. Thoughts (which are neurons firing) fire together over time and wire together in the shape of beliefs. If we are told we are messy or 'the naughty one', we believe it. If we notice ourselves struggling to concentrate during lessons we tell ourselves we can't do this or that. Our thought patterns become automatic and habitual and create beliefs which are often based on inaccurate thoughts, judgements and concerns. They often come from other people's thoughts, judgements and concerns or from our own self-fulfilling prophecies.

For example, as a child we might hear our parents refer to us being clumsy. We believe that we're clumsy and expect to be so.

This means, every time we trip over or drop something (which everyone does) it cements our belief that we are indeed clumsy. This expectation can ramp up our anxiety whenever we're in a situation which may need us to take care and pay attention, so we fall or slip and prove ourselves to be clumsy once again. The repeated thought of 'I'm clumsy' becomes a firm belief and a self-fulfilling prophecy. Only when we stop to question our beliefs, to seek evidence to dispute them, can we uncover the truth. Another way of looking at this long-held belief might be: 'I've been told since childhood that I'm clumsy, so I became so. However, I've noticed, when I slow down, breathe deeply and perform tasks, I'm actually no longer clumsy. In fact, I haven't dropped anything for months. I sometimes trip over, but I'm not particularly clumsy anymore. I'm not so clumsy after all.'

It's risky to challenge our own false beliefs; to question our false selves and uncover our true selves. But it is vital to living a good life. Sadly too many of us fear what the fall out might be. We fear rejection and we don't want to rock the boat. So we continue living a lie in order to keep us safe.

What we don't realise is that the rejection we fear is also based on false beliefs and concerns about a future which hasn't happened yet. We concoct worst case scenarios and crises in our heads, based on the judgements and concerns we've learned ourselves or been taught, yet these false future scenarios are based on false beliefs and false evidence.

Jumping to conclusions is a thinking trap most of us fall into. We assume that if we change in anyway, people will lose respect for us, or won't like or love us anymore. But how can we know that for sure? How can we know what will happen in the future when the future hasn't happened yet. It's all just prediction and assumption. When we begin to seek evidence to dispute our belief that nobody will like us if we change, we can prove that belief wrong. For example, if we're a parent and we assume our parents would no longer love or respect us if we chose a working role which suited us more than their expectations, we can look to our own children and wonder, would we love them any less if they chose to do something that made them happy rather than made us happy? No, we wouldn't. Nor would our own parents.

And yet these fears run deep.

False evidence appearing real

Susanne Jeffers in her book, *Feel The Fear and Do It Anyway* explains the concept of fear in a very potent way. She refers to fear as "FALSE EVIDENCE APPEARING REAL."

This makes so much sense because, ultimately, beliefs are the result of the stories we tell ourselves and the stories we've been told, for which we constantly gather evidence to support.

As such, fear is simply a fearful belief based on these stories and false evidence. Fear is the accumulation of false beliefs that we've been taught since childhood. Trans-generational beliefs that our parents and grandparents believed in: the should's and shouldn'ts, the do's and the don'ts.

But why were these should's and shouldn'ts, do's and don'ts taught to us?

The answer is deeper than any ethical or moral code, it is about control and avoidance and fear: to avoid evoking any feelings of blame, shame or judgement on the family; to avoid you bringing those feelings to the door of the home. This is something our parents feared and it's something we are conditioned to fear ourselves, and so we pass on those fears down the generations.

They are taught to us because they were taught to our parents before us and their parents before them. And so it goes on - conditioning handed down through the generations.

Control is safe and conforming is comfortable

And yet, whilst having a loving family is important, having a controlling family is different. When we have a controlling family we can become severely repressed by them. Sometimes control is borne out of love (to keep children safe, to get them to behave so they can go out into the world and remain safe). And yet some control can lead to repression as we bury our true selves under the demands of our family.

Early in our childhood, when we were free, we needed convincing that we ought to behave a certain way, to conform to a norm. Of course we need a moral and ethical code to live by but, in the plasticity of a child's mind, these messages became literal and the law. Once this programming was in place, we tried very hard to adhere to it, so as not to feel the rejection, disappointment or anger of the family towards us.

We don't want to disappoint our family. We crave love not rejection, we want love not anger, we desire acceptance and praise, not disappointment and criticism. That's human nature. And so we follow the should's and shouldn'ts as best we can.

If we ever did disobey the programming and we felt rejected, then we started to believe we were mad or bad or stupid or unlovable. We started to believe we weren't good enough, that it was our fault, for not behaving the way we should. We'd then berate ourselves and decide whether or not to continue with the behaviour that prevented us from feeling this way: a loop of pushing against the boundaries and beliefs, feeling bad, believing we were at fault and going in a 360 degree cycle, before deciding to conform again.

The truth was far less harsh. If we disobeyed the programming, if we spoke out of turn or failed to conform, this was simply part of our natural development as children. Pushing against boundaries is natural, it's how we learn. But, unless we were told that, we wouldn't know this truth. So we'd assume we were naughty and that would become our truth.

We either conform or we don't. But we pay the price of our freedom either way. If we conform, our true selves are buried. If we don't, we gain the labels and the rejection and we feel like we are losing in life. Either way, we lose.

This may sound bleak, but it's the truth for many people, who suffer from depression or anxiety and other mental health issues. Of course, for some, the truth is less dire as they grow out of their conforming behaviours and feel they are becoming more empowered, accepted not rejected.

The power of suggestion

For the conformists, in childhood it feels right to do as you are told, even if you know what you are told doesn't align with your own beliefs. And I'm not talking about stealing sweets from a shop, I am talking about expressing yourself in a way that you know ought to be ok, yet you're not allowed to.

Messages can be very covert too, often people don't realise they are being repressed because the repression can be given as a compliment.

For example, "Jane is very sensible; she never jumps on the furniture. She's a good girl."

Jane hears the compliment and says to herself, "Yep. I know how the world works, if I'm the good child, I'm lovable."

Conversely, John hears, "He's always naughty, he's such a nuisance! Why can't he be more like his sister?"

John says to himself, 'Oh well, I was just made this way. They don't love me, so I may as well carry on."

Both Jane and John have their identities now. The adults have been the script writers and the children play their parts. They've been told who to be, how to behave, what they should and shouldn't do.

Jane may want to be a little bit naughty sometimes and jump on the furniture. It looks fun! John may want to be good sometimes, but the parts are set and so are the beliefs. From this moment onward their lives will be directed by their beliefs around these parts that they are supposed to play, parts which may have little to do with who they truly are.

'Parts' is an operative word here, because we are only playing one part of us while the other parts of us never gets a chance to show up. Identical twins have told me, 'I am the pretty one, she is the brainy one.'

Yet they look exactly the same!

Neither is prettier and they're both intelligent in their own way, but that's what they've been told, so that's what they believe. They've been given false evidence so they may play their part in the game of life. That's the power of suggestion and belief.

Once those thoughts and suggestions have been repeated often enough those neural pathways run deep. Sufficiently so to believe falsities as truths, sufficiently so that we carve out our identities and choose how to respond to situations dependent on the part we have been given to play, depending on someone else's belief, depending on a lie.

As soon as the lie is believed it becomes a truth.

Later, Jane and John may begin to subconsciously numb any frustrated or angry feelings about their labels and having to play the parts they didn't have a choice in.

Surviving over thriving

This impasse can only be relieved when we take risks to change. Yet, more often than not, we are conditioned to see change in a negative way, and we are warned against it.

Normality is safe.

Keeping things as they are is safe.

Conforming is safe.

And our brains like safe, because they are wired to stay safe.

It's our survival instinct to stay so.

We don't relish risk or uncertainty for this very reason. When we consider changing or fret about the possibility of finding our true selves, we automatically question it, as we believe our friends and family might no longer be able to relate to us, so believe we'd have to get a whole set of new friends, or run away to some far away place where no one knows us and start all over again. Wrong! It's fear. False Evidence Appearing Real.

Who says friends will no longer be able to relate to us? This is based on more false beliefs! And so the perpetual loop of falsehoods continues. And, even if you did run away to start all over again, you'd still have the same beliefs and would find more people giving you reasons to stay just as you are. Either way, stick or twist, you won't want to change.

No, the only way to change and become your true self is to do something DIFFERENTLY. To question your beliefs and to reframe them, so you can respond in a different way to the way you've been conditioned.

We are neurologically wired to automatically give the same responses to others wherever we are until we do something else, until we do something different.

But what is that something different?

Curiosity killed the cat but freed the human

That something different is questioning with gentle curiosity. It's asking questions and considering the possibility that what you believe to be true is untrue, that what you believe to be right is wrong and that you have it within you to be the happiest truest you, once you've found your answers to these questions.

Only when you live your life through a lens of curiosity rather than conforming can you replace judgement with joy.

And here is something I know to be true. You deserve to feel joy. It's your birthright to be free and joyful.

Let me ask you a question:

How much do you think you are worth?

I have asked that question of many people. The answers vary, but those struggling with depression or anxiety tend to formulate their answers as follows:

"Well, I think I am a nice person. I'm a hard worker, I'm a manager now. I have a nice house in such and such a postcode and a decent car and we are doing alright."

This answer describes what someone does and what they have of value. It's based on an inherent belief which has come from their need to belong, to fit in, to keep up with the Jones's; a need to be the same or better than others.

I very rarely get an answer to do with how worthwhile the person feels about themselves or their life. It is rarely connected to joy. Nobody says, 'I'm so happy and content with my life.' Of course, those I pose this question to are coming to me for therapy, so it's unlikely they're completely happy with their lives. But I wonder how many people who don't come for therapy could say that last sentence?

And yet, to live in joy free from depression and anxiety is what we are all worth. This is how we can all feel, once we are free again.

Honesty is the best policy

The first step towards finding your true self is being as honest as you can about whatever you know is *not* bringing you joy.

Acknowledging and identifying areas of your life that drain you of your joy is an important step, because only when you highlight what is getting in the way of your thriving can you truly thrive. We'll explore more about how to hone in on what matters most and how to tune in to your true feelings in Chapter 7.

The second step towards finding your true self is to learn how to use the neuro-plasticity of your brain to reframe your thoughts and fine tune your thoughts into new beliefs that lead to your freedom.

This is because your thoughts are so often inaccurate, based on all of this trans-generational and peer to peer conditioning.

The most confused
we ever get is
when we try to
convince our heads
of something our
hearts know is a lie.

Karen Moning

CHAPTER 3
Thinking vs feeling

Thinking? Feeling? What's the difference?

Understanding the difference between thinking and feeling is the first step to removing the anaesthetic we subconsciously administered many years ago.

Because, thinking and feeling are not the same.

One is thought; the other is the precursor of emotion. One has the power to enable or disable; the other has the power to set us free.

Crucially, one leads to another. What we think determines what we believe and how we feel, which, in turn, determines how we act, react and respond. So, given the impact that thinking has on how we feel and what we do, what we think is of vital importance.

Thinking does not do feeling; it *causes* feeling, but it is not the same as feeling. In fact, thinking is often feeling's bully.

Remember John? On that fateful day at nursery, thinking told his 'Anger and Sadness': "do not do any overt feeling otherwise we will be nowhere - stop feeling and you'll stay safe."

Thinking bullied Feeling. "Repress those feelings otherwise we will not belong," it warned.

And John is not alone. Thinking often bullies feeling for all of us. Thinking feeds feeling with inaccurate negative thoughts which create consequential actions. For example, when we think a judgemental thought, such as 'I'll never be able to do such and such,' or 'I'm terrible at such and such.'

This makes us believe we are not good enough, which makes us feel disappointed, ashamed, guilty. This feedback loop of negativity all began with that thought. And yet, that thought may have minimal basis in reality. In fact, it is quite likely that, when we take that thought to court, we can find sufficient evidence to dispute it. For, with practice, it is likely that we could improve at whatever we think we're terrible at and, if we look deeper, we might find evidence to support the belief that we have, on occasion, been quite good at whatever we think we're terrible at.

Knowing your CBTs and ABCs

The problem is, our thoughts create our beliefs which become our mental schemas. So our thoughts and beliefs are very powerful. They have consequences. They determine how we feel and how we behave. As the Cognitive Behavioural Therapy ABC model suggests, our thoughts are in control of how we respond to setbacks in our lives and, essentially what we do next.

In this model:

A is the Adversity

B is the Belief

C is the Consequence.

So, let's say the Adversity (A) is that you don't get a management role you've applied for. If you are thinking pessimistically, you might think (and therefore believe) you didn't get the job because you're not good enough (B). Conversely, if you are thinking with realistic optimism, you might believe you didn't get the job because there were most likely a lot of applications and, although your skillset is strong in many of the required areas, you didn't have quite enough experience in a specific area (B).

The consequence of the first pessimistic belief of believing you're not good enough would be that you don't bother applying for management jobs and opt instead, for lower-paid jobs you know you can easily do (C). The consequence of the second more realistic and optimistic belief is that you sign up for a training course in the specific area in which your feel weaker, or continue to apply for management roles where that specific area is not a requirement (C).

Can you instantly see which consequence enables you and which disables you? There's a big difference and yet the action was created by that initial thought. The first thinking pattern of not being good enough results in an outcome of giving up at the first hurdle and applying for jobs which don't challenge or even appeal to you. And yet, the first thinking pattern is likely to be inaccurate, because of the inbuilt negativity bias that we, as humans, have. The actual likelihood is that you *are* good enough for the role, but so are lots of other applicants, some of whom may just have a slightly stronger CV due to more experience or qualification in a specific area that this particular job has specified.

Untrue thoughts

The truth, as scientific researchers and psychologists have discovered, is that many of our thoughts (especially the judgemental 'why' thoughts and the anxious future based 'what if' thoughts) are inaccurate.

Other times, thinking overrides our feelings and bullies feeling back into conforming to our conditioning. In this way, we think, 'I mustn't show I'm upset/disappointed/feeling anything' and we repress our feelings. As such, thinking can block us from releasing permission to ourselves to be free and live in joy.

Either way, thinking can cause us to return to the very things we are trying to break free from - being trapped in a world where we don't let our feelings flow or guide us and being trapped in a prison where our thoughts limit and restrict us.

And yet, these limiting actions are driven by thoughts which are not factually correct, they are often inaccurate, based on false expectations and judgements and conditioning (from peers, parents and the wider world at large).

So what does all this mean?

It means we shouldn't believe the first thought that pops into our head by default. Judgemental thoughts are often too harsh, while anxious worry thoughts are based on possibility rather than reality, on imagined future scenarios rather than on actual facts. Beliefs have a habit of being inflexible because they've been created as a result of repeating thoughts over and over again (that's how thoughts create neural pathways, which become beliefs). Indeed, with inaccurate thoughts and inflexible beliefs running around our heads, it's crucial to regain control and to be more flexible in our thinking.

To break free from the conditioning imprisoning us, we need to:

1. Tackle and shed our old inaccurate thought patterns and replace them with a new belief system based on facts and our own truth, rather than other peoples' truth or our own misguided reality; to cultivate thinking patterns and beliefs which are accurate and flexible.

2. Allow our feelings to guide us. Tap into our intuition, free up our feelings to become our guide and enable them to flow, as emotions.

Reframing our beliefs and using, what psychologists call 'Real-time Resilience' to speak to talk back to our inaccurate negative thoughts is the next step in removing that anaesthetic, so we'll explore how to talk back to our negative thoughts and reframe beliefs in Chapter 6.

In the meantime, it's useful to understand the kind of thinking traps that our habitual thought patterns tend to imprison us in.

Thinking traps

Resilience researchers and authors of *The Resilience Factor*, Reivich and Shatte give some great examples of the kind of thinking traps we all tend to fall into from time to time.

JUMPING TO CONCLUSIONS:

Humans assume. We think we know what a situation means, despite not having any evidence to support our assumptions.

That's why jumping to conclusions is such a widely shared thinking trap, which so many of us fall into. In fact, most of the thinking traps listed here are some form of jumping to conclusions.

But there are antidotes to these thinking traps.

The antidote to this thinking trap is to slow down, pause and notice what you're thinking, then look for the evidence to support or deny that belief. For example, you may send a lengthy message to someone requesting their advice and receive a one-sentence reply. In which case you may jump to the conclusion that the recipient of your heart-felt message doesn't care about you and only cares about themselves.

Yet, if you look for the evidence to support or refute that belief, you would likely discover that they do care. Perhaps they are in the middle of something at work and don't yet have the time to send a lengthy response. Maybe they'll respond more fully later. Perhaps, when you take the time to reflect back on your interactions with this person, you'll recollect many times when they've devoted ample time to comforting, supporting and encouraging you.

TUNNEL VISION:

We fall into this thinking trap when we hone in on small insignificant details and ignore the more relevant ones.

The antidote to this thinking trap is to widen your perspective and seek more information so you can consider what you may have missed. For example, let's say you send off your resume in hopeful anticipation for a job you are perfect for, but you notice a few spelling or grammatical errors. You may focus on the fact you've made some errors and come to the conclusion that you've blown your opportunity, rather than considering the bigger picture of how your skills and experience listed in your resume demonstrate you are perfect for the job. Not being able to see the wood for the trees can create a pessimistic view of a situation when we haven't considered all the information about it.

OVER-GENERALISING:

This is a common thinking trap which happens when we decide or believe something based on one situation, rather than considering alternative possibilities and explanations. For example, you might judge someone as being lazy or unmotivated because they fail to meet your expectations around effort or don't respond instantly to a request. However, what if you considered other possibilities and looked at behaviour which might explain why the person you're judging has acted in a certain way. This flexible thinking would give you a more accurate picture. That's the antitdote to over-generalisation - to consider specific behaviour which might explain the situation.

MAGNIFYING AND MINIMISING:

Another common thinking trap is to blow things out of proportion so they appear far worse than they actually are. This happens when we minimise the positive details and magnify the negative ones, marring our accurate evaluation of events.

The antidote to this thinking is to find the good and be more balanced and even-handed in our perception of events. For example, you might assume you've done a bad job when you receive one piece of negative feedback from a customer about your workshop, despite receiving 12 pieces of glowing feedback explaining how useful they found it. It's human nature to focus on the negative.

We owe it to ourselves to find the good in order to think more accurately.

PERSONALISATION and EXTERNALISATION:

We fall into this thinking trap when we blame ourselves for causing a problem or for failing to solve it. Attributing blame means we are not considering other possible reasons for an adversity. So the antidote to this thinking trap is to look outward rather than inward; to consider how other circumstances may have contributed to the situation.

For example, if you find out that a friend who confided in you has slipped into depression, you may conclude that you weren't helpful enough and blame yourself for not being able to lift their spirits when, in actual fact, you listened. Their illness isn't about you. Other circumstances are more likely to have contributed to them feeling down, mostly what they are experiencing in their job, at home, and so on.

Similarly, when we blame others for causing a problem or failing to solve it, we aren't considering our own involvement. So the antidote to externalisation is to look inward rather than outward; to consider how we may have contributed to the situation too.

MIND READING:

We all tend to assume we know what other people are thinking and/or expect other people to know what we are thinking, even when they or we haven't expressed ourselves.

The antidote to this is to speak up, either by asking questions to find out what people are thinking rather than assume we know without being informed, and to express ourselves so we can clearly explain what we are thinking so others don't have to guess or assume inaccurately. There is no point believing something to be true based on guess work or assumption.

For example, if a friend is quiet you might assume they think you're talking too much when, in actual fact, they may have a lot going on in their life right now and may be distracted or, they may simply be interested in what you're saying and prefer to listen.

Awareness of thinking traps enables us to catch ourselves falling into them and shift our thought processes to step over them, which we'll explore in more detail in Chapter 6. For now, leaning into the knowledge that it is possible to change your thinking and, in doing so, change HOW YOU FEEL!

Now isn't that a welcome fact?

Trying to protect us from harm

Having read all of the rubbish that thinking puts us through, you might be feeling annoyed at your thinking. However, rather than feel angry at our thoughts for misleading us in this way, we should view our brains with compassion. You see, we have an inbuilt negativity bias for a reason. It's just trying to protect us. So let's forgive 'thinking' for it cleverly anaesthetising our feelings and acting as our guardian. For that's just the way it's wired, and for good reason.

First, our negative bias is there to protect us from harm by sparking the fight or flight response and second by comparing us to others, its intention is to get us to up our game, so we can survive. Back when we lived in caves and in tribes, this was necessary - we needed a critical brain to alert us to the fact we needed to improve and we needed a cautious brain to alert us to the fact that the rustling bushes may well be hiding a sabre tooth tiger. In those days, it was better to be cautious and risk the embarrassment of the rustling bushes being nothing but a small rodent, than the alternative, which was death by sabre tooth. By triggering our fight or flight response, we were ready to respond accordingly to danger.

Second, we've been conditioned to think that showing emotion is a weakness, so our brain bullies us away from feeling to protect us from all the repressed, depressed feelings that we mistakenly think may lead us to breakdown.

Thankfully, when we realise these truths of neuro-science, we can uncover our own personal truths and the truth will set us free. And so will our feelings.

Feeling is your SatNav

Unlike thought, feeling is truth. Feeling is knowledge. As such, feelings provide the all important SatNav system to guide us in the right direction. Yes, feelings can be influenced by inaccurate thoughts, but the feelings themselves are real. But you know that already.

Thoughts that are conditioned will remain conditioned until they have something else to refer to. Feeling is the more accurate guide to what you want. How many times have we heard someone say "I had a hunch about that," or "I had a gut feeling". And how many times have we made a decision which went wrong, so we say to ourselves, "I knew I shouldn't have gone ahead I had a gut feeling."

Now here or nowhere

If you notice the words above *'now here'* as separate entities, this is when you are focussed in the moment. Now put the words together and you get *'nowhere'*, this is what happens when you are not fully focussed on your thoughts and feelings which can make you feel chaotic and confused.

"A gut feeling is actually every cell in your body making a decision,"

Deepak Chopra

If you feel lost, there is one way to find yourself and find your way back to your rightful path - to feel. You have to feel in order to find yourself. Feeling is your satellite navigation system back to yourself, back to your truth, back to what you want and back to who you are. This means, to find out who you truly are, you must return to feeling, you must hone in on your heart. The only way to get somewhere is to return to feeling and return to yourself and to what you want from this precious life of yours.

Too many people have been lost, and in order to numb their uncomfortable feelings, have turned to drink, over-eating, self harm or Obsessive Compulsive Disorder (OCD).

We want the F factor to stand for FREEDOM not FATALITY. So please don't let these negative reactions ruin your life.

Instead, choose life, choose feeling, because returning to feeling is the most richness a human being can have. Remember if you numb all the bad feelings you numb all the joy too! If you numb feeling, your reactions become robotic and your life inauthentic with no integrity; without your heart's desire and real feelings leading the way forward. And if you ignore feelings and let your thoughts rule your reactions, you end up making decisions based on inaccurate beliefs which just don't serve you.

So the head (thinking) and the heart or gut (feeling) must come together in order to create an accurate SatNav. To get where you want to be, you need a compass and a map.

When we see feeling as our compass, showing us which way we want to go and thinking (accurate, flexible thinking rather than inaccurate irrational thinking) as our map, helping us explore where to go and who to enlist to help us get there, we can escape the trap we've been caught in for all these years and move forward, onward and upward.

Positive thinking vs position emotion and negative thinking vs negative emotion

When discussing the difference between THINKING vs FEELING, it's crucial to explore the difference between positive thinking and position feeling/emotion and between negative thinking and negative feeling/emotion.

A lot has been written about positive thinking, but it's not the same as developing our reserves of positive emotion (feeling). Similarly, while negative thinking can trap us and lead us to react in ways which don't best serve us, negative emotions can be useful and have a surprisingly positive impact on our lives. If only we know how to use them.

Think positive

Positive thinking is about having an optimistic and hopeful outlook rather than a pessimistic and hopeless one.

Pessimism and optimism are two types of explanatory style, i.e. how we explain the reason circumstances happen, whether those circumstances are good or bad. As Professor Martin Seligman, a founding father of positive psychology discovered after 30 years of study, those with a pessimistic explanatory style tend to see setbacks as their fault (personalised), as long-lasting (permanent) and as undermining everything they do (pervasive). Whereas, those with an optimistic explanatory style tend to see setbacks as down to external circumstances, as temporary and as specific (so not their fault and able to overcome).

And, when it comes to successes, those with a pessimistic explanatory style tend to see successes as down to external circumstances, as temporary and as specific (so nothing to do with them and unlikely to be repeatable), whereas those with an optimistic explanatory style tend to see successes as personal, long-lasting and pervasive (so absolutely to do with their own effort and likely to be sustainable).

Thankfully, because of neuro-plasticity and the ability, with practice for us to shift our thinking styles, even the most hardened pessimist can begin to see the causes of their successes and setbacks differently. We'll explore more about shifting our thinking styles from pessimistic to optimistic in Chapter 6.

In the meantime, this factual data discovered by scientists and psychologists after years of studies, should serve as evidence that our THINKING styles are learned and, as such we can unlearn them and learn better ways of thinking. In doing so we can provide ourselves with a more accurate map to get us back on track.

Even better news is that both positive thinking and positive emotions:

- improve our lives by enabling us to feel better (about ourselves and about what happens to us),

- help us think more clearly

- improve our problem-solving abilities

- help us to bounce back from adversity more readily.

Here's how.

Broaden and build your thinking power and resilience

Dr Barbara Fredrickson has discovered after decades of research into positive emotion that negative thinking traps narrow our focus and lead to inaccurate thoughts and beliefs. Worrying actually makes us more likely to make irrational emotional decisions rather than rational ones based on facts.

This means, when we question our thoughts we can broaden our thinking and improve our problem-solving abilities, cultivating a more accurate, flexible and helpful thought process.

When it comes to resilience, the more accurate, flexible and helpful our thought process is, the better able we are to recover well.

So:

- BROADEN - POSITIVE THINKING not only does this provide us with hope. It also opens our minds to possibilities and solutions to problems. Whereas NEGATIVE THINKING closes down our rational brain and disables our problem-solving abilities.

- BUILD - POSITIVE EMOTION (positive feeling) such as gratitude and love can be stored away in our wellness reserves and used, like currency, when we most need them. They are useful in enabling us to cope.

So you can see that positive thinking gives us hope and positive emotion helps us to cope!

Emotional early warning system

There is another crucial consideration when understanding the difference between thinking and feeling. Now, and this is IMPORTANT, although we know NEGATIVE THINKING can restrict our ability to respond well (affecting our cognitive ability and closing down our ability to think clearly/logically), NEGATIVE EMOTIONS can actually sometimes serve us. That said, we don't want our emotional brain to lead the way as it gets in the way of rationale. But we can learn a lot from our negative emotions.

What's more, there's a lot of pressure today to 'don't worry, be happy', but there is a paradox in positivity in that this pressure to be happy can have the opposite effect and make us more unhappy if we feel we're not living up to societal/familial/our own expectations. This is even more relevant when you take the rise of social media into consideration, as we compare our unedited worst show reel to everyone else's best unfiltered show reel.

It's important that we give ourselves permission to be human and feel and express our feelings and emotions. For all emotions are useful, even negative ones, such as anger/sadness, as they act as an early warning system and catalysts to shift our actions. Yes, difficult emotions signal the need for change and provide useful data. They give us an important early warning system.

Some negative thoughts can motivate us and thus serve us. For example, if you think you're unlikely to win a race, that thought might serve to motivate you to practice more and work harder to achieve your goal of winning. In that case, it may well serve you. Similarly, if a worry is about an immediate life-threatening event, such as a fast car approaching, it will serve you by preventing you from stepping into the road.

However, that's the only caveat. If a thought or belief causes you to worry and get stressed and disables you, it's not serving you.

Consider a belief you currently hold. Ask yourself:

1. Is my thinking based on fact? Are these thoughts absolutely true? How can I be sure?

2. How does this belief make me feel and react? What do I do or not do as a consequence of that belief? Does it help me to achieve my goals? Does it serve me?

3. Does my thinking help me feel and behave the way I want to feel and behave?

4. How might I feel and behave without that belief?

Remember, the good news is that we can cultivate optimistic thinking by identifying our mind chatter, collecting evidence to dispute our beliefs and talking back to our more pessimistic thoughts. We can also reduce our worrying thoughts by gaining perspective. See Chapter 6.

In the meantime, while negative thinking (judgements and worries, for example) doesn't tend to serve us, and can bully feeling and negatively impact our actions, reactions and, well, our lives, negative emotions can serve us.

How feeling bad can lead to feeling good

In this sense, depression, anxiety, OCD, alcoholism, eating disorders can all be useful to us. As such they can actually become our other 'F' factor - our friend.

Yes, you read correctly, depression and anxiety and discontent can be our wake-up call and our friend.

"Wait...What?" I hear you say! "How can you call my depression/anxiety/addiction my friend? It's terrible and it makes me feel terrible".

Yes it does, but in doing so, it is alerting you to the fact that SOMETHING NEEDS TO CHANGE. Rather than being the friend who tells you what you want to hear (like unrealistic optimism) your negative emotions are acting as the friend who tells you the truth.

Depression, anxiety, addiction are all saying, 'yes, my friend, this situation is making you feel terrible, so we need to accept what we can't change and change what we can, to help you feel better.'

"Insanity is doing the same thing over and over and expecting different results."

In this way, these ailments provide us with a wake-up call - they are that friend who grabs us by the shoulders and shakes us, saying, 'this means you need to do something differently! You deserve better than this!' And let me tell you something, that friend is right!

Inherent in the depression is a wake-up call to our true nature - it's our built-in alarm bell. It's our early warning system. It's our lighthouse giving us a chance to stop on this route to prevent us from crashing into the rocks of anxiety and downward spirals under the waves of depression - so we may change course and sail to freedom! When you look at depression and anxiety and all the negative emotions and feelings which have been caused as a result of the negative thinking that have sewn the seeds of depression and anxiety, you can see them as USEFUL, helpful warning bells that protect you from sinking deeper.

Your feelings are your lighthouse and your choices are your life raft because together, they can then guide you away from the rocks. They can alert you to the notion that you need to change your thinking patterns (which is absolutely possible).

Therefore what is in our way is our way

The obstacles show us which route we need to take, the answers are in the problem.

It's so important for us to give ALL feelings a seat at the table; to give ourselves permission to feel. Because FEELING is real, thinking isn't.

Yes, you can give fear a seat at a table, you can give anger and sadness and worry and jealousy and guilt a seat. You can even give them a voice. Let them speak, hear them out, listen to them in all of their brutality, and let them help you figure out what you want and what feels right. Just don't give negative emotions the driving seat or the final say.

Conversely, give your positive emotions - gratitude, love, awe - the driving seat. Feel them and hear them and let them help you figure out what you want and what feels right, so you can navigate your way through the negative emotions and learn what matters most to you and what is getting in the way of what matters most - tap into your feelings to understand which direction you ought to travel in.

Then, once we emerge, having reminded us to make changes, our feelings turn to us and say, 'hey, that old stuff is over, now let me out.' And out they flow.

Emotional flow

What then of Emotion?

Notice the word 'emotion' has 'motion' in it, which means 'to move'.

Emoting is the processing of feeling. To cry is emoting your sadness, to laugh is emoting your joy, to scream or shout is emoting your anger from being abused or disrespected.

Now, in general, we think of being angry as an emotion to avoid. Or we think of crying as a weakness. Yet there are health values to emoting your anger. It can reduce heart conditions, relieve stress and other physical ailments, while emoting your sadness gives you an opportunity to release cortisol (the stress hormone) through your tears.

What's more, it's possible to express anger with love. Many of us have seen anger at work when it has become nasty and loud and frightening, so that is how we view anger. Few of us may have witnessed anger expressed with love (soft and strong).

Expressing your displeasure with someone by telling them in a firm but fair fashion, "your comment/behaviour upset me the other day because I've noticed it matters to me whether you think I'm doing a good job or not, and I don't want our relationship to suffer. I'm sensing an uncomfortable atmosphere so I'd really like to clear this up, because I value our relationship. Can we?"

In this model you are saying you value the relationship and so you want the relationship to be caring enough and loving enough to be able to freely express yourselves.

The model we are used to is one of blame vs defensiveness "Grrrr! You behaved like this that and the other and I am done with you"... "No I did not! How dare you accuse me of this that and the other. You're no better, you did this that and the other last week," and so on and so forth!

Using this terminology does not give participants in the valued relationship a chance to understand what was really going on and caused a rupture. Yet, rather than automatically going to our default model (of judgement / defence) we can still express ourselves, but with compassion for ourselves and the other person in the relationship.

Anger with love

In this way, anger with love is the way forward. However, it's vital that it is expressed not repressed, otherwise we end up with the proverbial elephant in the room. The atmosphere changes, snide comments are made, sarcasm is used and the elephant just gets fed.

When we move our emotion, we carefully ride the elephant, rather than letting it run amok. As such, anger with love results in healing rather than wreckage.

Because our feelings need somewhere to go. We can sit with our feelings and acknowledge them, really FEEL our FEELINGS and we can let them flow through us by emoting them.

Or we can ignore them, stifle them, try to push them down or numb them. When we do the latter we stay trapped, our feelings repressed. When we do the former we set ourselves free, our feelings expressed.

By returning to feeling we free ourselves.

We move from repression to expression, from imprisonment to freedom.

A core truth in psychology is that our thoughts become beliefs and our beliefs affect our feelings, which impact our behaviour. Literally what we do is directly impacted by what we think and believe and by how we feel.

In order to find our truth and regain our freedom then, we need to focus some attention on our thoughts, beliefs and feelings.

So, about that...

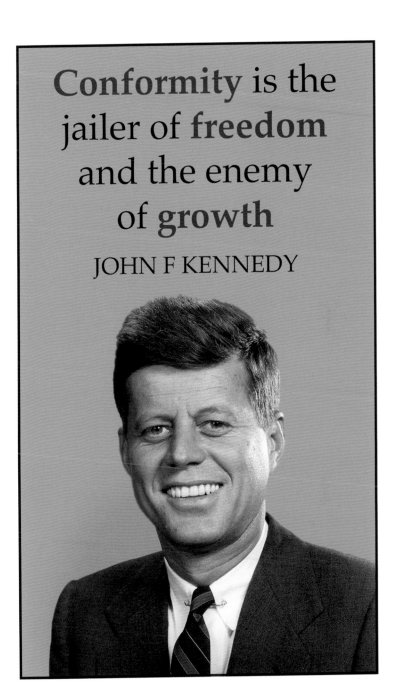

Conformity is the jailer of **freedom** and the enemy of **growth**

JOHN F KENNEDY

CHAPTER 4
From repression to expression: feel your way to freedom

Being armoured up is getting us down

Masking our feelings is something we all do to some extent.

Sometimes this is to protect others from seeing our true feelings; from knowing how we genuinely feel. We worry about them worrying about us.

Sometimes this is because of the image we want to convey to others that 'everything is awesome'. How others perceive us is important to us humans. What others think of us matters (because being held in high regard was important to our survival when we lived in tribes). And, because showing emotion, despite being natural and useful and beautiful, has been cast in societal stories as weak, we mask our feelings and self-anaesthetise as a result of our fears (which, by the way, are based on false evidence/inaccurate thoughts and beliefs).

We believe that showing our feelings might give the game away! Our fears of being 'found out', of being disliked, perceived to be weak, worried about, letting down our guard, and so on enforce our need to ensure that our mask doesn't slip.

Masking our feelings is part of the armour we put up around ourselves over time. We don't have this armour when we are 'born free'. We build it up gradually so our mask keeps our feelings hidden and our emotions buried deep inside.

The first time we armoured up and began to numb our feelings was when our opinion was first denied or rejected and we started to feel unimportant, unloved or rejected. That was when we started the process of numbing. Some refer to this numbing process as building a wall around their heart and losing their feeling.

What are you afraid of?

No wonder it can feel scary to remove the wall, because behind that wall could be all the grief and disappointment and pain that we have never felt. If we remove our armour, won't it all come flooding out? Clients have said to me, 'I can't feel all the pain. For if I do I will start to cry and disappear in a flood and I will never be able to function again!' That is the fear. Let's remind ourselves of what fear is: False Evidence Appearing Real. We falsely think that by opening those flood gates, we'll break or destroy ourselves. And yet the converse is true.

News Update: Feelings won't break you, they will FREE you!

The notion that feeling our feelings and allowing our emotions to flow will break us is a myth. Because releasing feelings does not break you, it frees you. The clue is in the word - feeling. We need to feel them. We are meant to. That's what they are for. They're not meant to be hidden away and locked up behind layer upon layer of armour. We're not meant to mask our emotions.

You see, the truth is, feeling and releasing your feelings won't destroy you, because they never did! When you were born and free, expressing your emotions alerted your caregivers that you needed something (food, warmth, love, sleep, etc). You expressed your needs via your emotions. Doing so didn't harm you or destroy you; it empowered you by revealing what you needed. You still need to do that. Feelings are our navigation system to demonstrate what we need. If we feel sad, we need hope or a hug, we need love or something to look forward to and lift us up. If we feel angry, we need to move our bodies or use our anger as a catalyst to enforce change. If we feel guilty, we need to right a wrong or commit to learning from our mistakes. Feelings guide our response and the right action. (Whereas, thought often guides the wrong reaction, as explored in the previous chapter).

So we should listen to our feelings.

Until you set the repressed feelings free, you'll carry them with you and remain depressed.

Expressed feelings are the route to freedom.

Repression = depression.

Expression = freedom.

Being emotional is GOOD not BAD!

In reading this book, you have taken the first step to releasing the shackles of the conditioning which makes you think (wrongly) that feeling is bad when, in actual fact, feeling is a vital part of what it means to be human and those who feel and express their true feelings are more likely to live good, happy and successful lives, because they are free from those shackles.

Please don't cry!

But it's not our fault we've armoured up in this way. Society, family and peers have conditioned us not to cry. From childhood, our parents, or friends or teachers have said, 'please don't cry'.

Often this is not even because of the perception of crying as weak, but because the person asking you not to cry doesn't like to see you upset, because they care about you. 'Please don't cry', sounds like a comforting request to 'your thinking' and yet, what they are really saying is, 'I don't like to see you upset; I want to help you feel better?' Of course, all we hear is 'don't cry' or 'don't express your emotions' and we are conditioned to stop. Remember, that's all fear does, it just says 'stop', which is not a productive way to flourish and grow.

Stopping our emotions from flowing stunts our growth.

It would be far more helpful to enable and accept the expression of emotion by honouring and empathising and saying, 'I can see you're feeling sad,' or 'Ouch, that really hurts doesn't it?' or even 'Have a good cry, let those feelings out,' perhaps followed by, 'Let's see if I can help you feel better.' By removing the don'ts and the dislike, we remove the restriction and repression.

Arrested development - Anaesthetising feelings

And yet, the status quo is what I call 'arrested emotional development' as we are so often prevented from expressing our true emotions.

Other times we are told not to cry because others cannot deal with our expression of feeling, so we find ourselves having to anaesthetise the feelings in order to survive.

In this instance, when they say 'please don't cry', the person is really saying, 'please don't express your emotions, because I don't know how to manage mine, and it's making me feel uncomfortable.' As a result of severe conditioning, emotions can make people who repress theirs the most feel uncomfortable when others express theirs. So they ask you to stop. Not only has the conditioning caused them to struggle to express their own emotions, they can't handle it when other people express theirs either.

As a result, the person doing the crying inherently realises they are making someone else uncomfortable so, tries to cheer up, repressing their feelings again. The repressed feelings causes the repression to continue. The repressed person passes the repression baton to the next person and so it continues - this relay of repression. A trans-generational baton in some cases.

With this covert message of 'please don't cry because I cannot handle it', thinking takes over. 'Thinking' says to 'feeling' "Yes I am in charge and if you get out of the way feeling I will look stronger and more in control."

This desire to feel in control rather than to lose control of our emotions guides us, instead of our feelings showing us what we really need in that moment.

We may feel like losing control is the biggest thing to fear when, in truth, losing our way, our route forward, by dismissing what our emotions are telling us we need, **that's the bigger loss!**

Other times we don't want to upset our mum, dad, partner, boss so we switch off our feelings. Or perhaps, when you first behaved in a way that visibly upset your parents you decided upsetting others did not feel good, so you arrested those feelings and numbed them.

Fast forward into adulthood and when our partner, boss or friend hurts our feelings, rather than saying, 'you hurt me' and having a truthful grown-up discussion about it where you honour each others' feelings, what tends to happen is a couple of developmentally arrested 'children' have a fight. This can still happen with people in later life who become very cantankerous and revert to their repressed 'terrible twos'.

The truth is, even if someone tried to get you to adhere to their way of being, they probably thought it was for your own well being. After all, they were probably indoctrinated too.

Take my own parents, for example. They had come through a war and lost many friends and relatives. Anaesthetising their feelings was a coping strategy. Similarly, generations before theirs had many struggles; ones we fortunately don't have these days.

So, rather than blame them for not showing their feelings, or allowing us to feel ours, we can approach this with compassion. When we tell ourselves, if only things had been different in our past, we are only imprisoning ourselves in the role of victim. Blame doesn't get us anywhere closer to finding our truth.

For example, if your mother, father, brother or lover was not able to love you in the way you wanted, if they left you, it could be because they were finding life so difficult that they left themselves.

As human beings we cannot authentically love others until we love ourselves and so many people don't love themselves, which makes it hard for them to show love to others.

The point is, the repression of feelings is indoctrinated as:

- A coping and controlling strategy (which doesn't work because feelings, especially repressed ones, resurface).
- A way of preventing others from seeing our true, vulnerable, emotional selves; a fear based on false evidence that we'd somehow lose respect if we let our

masks slip and revealed our true selves. Yet the opposite is true. We like and respect people who are true to themselves, who show up with integrity and who bravely reveal their own vulnerabilities. We admire them!

We are repressing our feelings based on false evidence. This is a sad fact of modern life, but it is also an ironic one given the scientific truth that expression, rather than repression, does us the world of good.

Boys have feelings too!

As a general rule boys have been asked not to feel more than girls, and the person making this request to stop crying is reinforcing the message that showing emotions is weak. When people tell their children, 'boys don't cry', that's incredibly damaging for boys and men, who are conditioned to repress their emotions. The extent of this repression has been linked to the rise in male suicide. It's that serious.

Trans-generationally boys have been told not to feel their feelings for such a long time. If boys have felt their feelings, the general consensus has been it is 'sissy' for boys to feel. This is a prime example of well-intended yet unfortunately harmful conditioning.

This conditioning and repressing message from 'thinking' can create irritation and obsession and anger that mustn't be expressed so is repressed instead. It then often comes out in feeling passive and then outbursts of aggression. After the outburst, guilt usually follows and we bow down to thinking again.

Soft front strong back = True courage

Let's us be clear here - crying can be strong! Some of the most passionate freedom fighters of our time had to feel strongly and passionately to set us free!

Crying can act as a catalyst for change - for making bold moves, and that's courage epitomised.

And, because our world has normalised the repression of feelings, telling someone that you are hurting and have feelings about it is especially brave and strong.

Yet still, crying vs conditioning is an ongoing battle.

Your conditioning will likely disagree with the notion that crying is a courageous emotional move, but I invite you to think about how strong it is to say that you are vulnerable? Most people want to hide their vulnerability. Most people feel like a child when they show their vulnerability.

Feeling vulnerable feels uncomfortable but, as Brené Brown, Research Professor on shame says, it also feels like courage:

Says Brené, "Vulnerability sounds like truth and feels like courage. Truth and courage aren't always comfortable, but they're never weakness."

"Owning our story can be hard but not nearly as difficult as spending our lives running from it," says Brené. "Embracing our vulnerabilities is risky but not nearly as dangerous as giving up on love and belonging and joy - the experiences that make us the most vulnerable. Only when we are brave enough to explore the darkness will we discover the infinite power of our light."

The norm is to want to avoid being judged for showing feelings of shame and embarrassment. We are not keen on being judged. And yet, when you choose to hide your vulnerability, that's inauthentic and dishonest and, let's be honest, that's the easy way; that's playing safe. Having the strength to show your vulnerable human side takes courage and integrity, just like Brené suggests - the most beautiful experiences make us vulnerable and take courage but they are worth it. And, as such, contrary to popular belief, it FEELS GOOD, once you take that first shaky step towards your true self, towards home!

Yes, it feels uncomfortable at first (due to our conditioning) but it also feels real and again, contrary to popular belief, when we do show up in a vulnerable way, people respond well to us. People show us empathy and support and love. They feel like they can relate to us, because they feel the same (even if they don't yet have the courage to express it or share their own vulnerability yet).

If we fear what people might think and that fear stops us from letting our guard down, removing our armour and stepping into our true vulnerability and expressing our true feelings, what if those people hold us in even higher regard when we do so, because they feel the same? We don't usually think that way but you can earn more respect by being true to yourself, by being vulnerable and emotional, than you can from armouring up, hiding your true self away and repressing your emotions like a robot.

If you are feeling hurt or attacked in some way, isn't it a shame to be made unable to say so. When this becomes the case, your world becomes a lie and you repress all your feelings again.

The good news is, you have what it takes to set your repressed feelings free. You have the courage inside you. In fact, it took more effort and restraint to carry them and shield them away than to do what is the natural order of things - to express them.

When you bring the 'F' factor (feelings) back, you turn that LIE into LIFE.

And I can assure you, it is far better to live LIFE in full expression and feeling across the whole spectrum of our emotions, than it is to live a LIE where we mask our true feelings.

Be grateful for feeling tearful

The problem is, we associate crying with weakness and hurt. Yet tears are signposts of something that is upsetting you in the moment or of something unresolved and not expressed from the past. As such they provide you with the opportunity to free yourself from past upsets.

As explained in more detail in the book, *A Course In Miracles*, often times, when we are upset, we are not upset for the reason that we think we are.

We could have felt a similar emotion, like abandonment by a partner or a colleague in the here and now that triggered a similar emotion that you may have felt as a child. An angry outburst could become more volatile than it should because you have stored old anger that has not been released. That's why we have to express our emotions from now on at the time of the event so it can be released. The analogy I would use is process emotions so they can't build to feeling like a tsunami or a volcanic eruption.

Tears or anger often come from the internal hurt young child, thus serving as a reminder of an old feeling that has never been expressed; a ghost of a feeling that has been hidden a long time ago. I refer to this as an emotional developmental arrest: a time in our development when our heart stopped feeling due to anaesthetising our feelings.

Once we acknowledge we have hidden grief, embarrassment, rejection from the past, we are free to choose how to manage it in an adult way in the future. Then, just as a heart beating pumps blood round our bodies, our brain can start releasing our emotions and freeing us from all that built-up locked-in pain.

What's more, when we cry, our tears release the stress hormone cortisol, so crying literally enables us to physically get rid of the stress as it pours out of us via our tears; a very healthy response to sadness, which makes us feel better.

Carrying the repressed baggage of the past saps your strength which is needed to build your future! Letting our repressed feelings go gives us energy, so we may face our future more readily.

Pay to release your pain or pay to hold onto it - you decide

If you feel that you've had to repress a lot of hurt feelings from abuse or ill treatment in the past, enlisting the help of a therapist may be necessary. For, sometimes the hurt inner child just needs a witness to hear the pain, because it wasn't heard years ago. In this way, investing in yourself is a better investment than silver or gold.

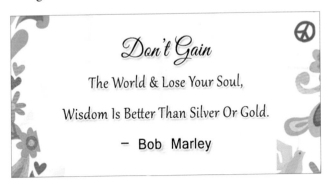

Don't Gain

The World & Lose Your Soul,

Wisdom Is Better Than Silver Or Gold.

− Bob Marley

When you see the self-investment of therapy in this way you won't ever tell yourself you can't afford the therapy, because you'll see instead that you can't afford not to.

Indeed, either way you'll pay. If you have a history of hidden hurt which you choose to keep hidden and repress your feelings, you'll risk paying with poor mental health. Or you can choose to pay to have someone help you release your prior pain and, in doing so, set yourself free.

Paying for things you can't enjoy because you are depressed is a waste of money. Investing in yourself and your freedom to live your best possible life is not. When you go and express your pain, your life will no longer be taken hostage by the past and you will experience the freedom you deserve.

As well as freeing yourself from darkness you'll be able to step into the light - by giving yourself permission to feel the difficult feelings you'll find an added bonus that you'll also start to magnify the good feelings again.

Because anaesthetic is not selective.

Turn the light back on!

A major problem with anaesthetising our feelings is that, although we only ever intended to numb the emotions which caused us or others hurt or pain, we didn't realise that by applying anaesthetic to our feelings, we diluted them all. Because, the thing with emotions is, we can't selectively numb them.

Rather than just numbing the feelings of rejection and hurt and keeping the feelings of joy and fun, we've accidentally diluted our ability to feel the good feelings as intensely. We've numbed the lot.

Subsequently, the process of numbing our feelings has not only dimmed our darkness, but it has dimmed our light too. And, the darkness only reappears years down the line, as a result of repression, in the form of depression.

If you have ever been depressed you may know that you have felt numb to EVERYTHING. For example, someone may say *"Good Morning"* to you and you reciprocate the same *"good morning"* in a cheery voice but, deep inside, you are saying *"just go away I don't feel like it is a good morning at all".*

Someone could even impart some tragic news to you and you feign the empathy. Indeed, no one would know that you are not sincere. But you know. So you start to feel that you are not a nice person and that, if people really knew you, they wouldn't like you, in fact you don't like you.

And so you feel like a fraud.

Sadly when this downward spiral starts, people do not believe that anyone likes them and that their friends and families would be better off without them. But this is never true. Nobody would ever be better off without you.

The downward spiral sometimes can lead to hopeless and helpless and worthless feelings.

This is not your fault; it's something that has happened over time. And, thankfully, you can switch the light back on, whenever you want to.

You can step into the recovery room and let the anaesthetic wear off.

It's perfectly natural to feel terrified about letting the numbness wear off for fear of hurting again. But feeling pain is better than feeling NOTHING, because, when you open the door to your pain, you also open to door to your joy.

"A life without feeling is like a world without light."

So many people have, like John mentioned in Chapter 1 and I and maybe like you, repressed their feelings for a myriad of different reasons. There are billions of stories, but only one spectrum of human emotions, ranging from love to hate and guilt to frustration. Fear gets in the way of us leaning in to feel them.

But you need your light to shine and you cannot do that when your light is switched off!

If you still fear opening the flood gates of pain, consider this...

Post Traumatic Growth

Scientists have found that the majority of people who experience trauma and adversity in their life bounce back but, not only that, many people also bounce forward. This is known as Post Traumatic Growth and means it's possible to grow, because we've experienced adversity not despite it.

In fact, they found that encountering obstacles and painful moments can actually be useful. They discovered, in order to truly thrive, we need to experience hardships because, each time we do, these adversities strengthen us by showing us that we can cope. Let that sink in, the notion that setbacks actually strengthen us, as per that famous 'Nietsche' phrase about *'what doesn't break us makes us stronger'*.

As Cheryl Rickman points out in her book, *The Little Book of Resilience*, five psychological shifts were found by scientists to be common among those who'd experienced PTG. They experienced greater personal strength, greater appreciation, deeper relationships, renewed sense of meaning in life and a renewed sense of new possibilities. _

Says Cheryl, "This personal process of change in how people thought and related to the world in the aftermath of the trauma is what led to the Post Traumatic Growth, rather than the trauma itself. Reports of these growth experiences far outweigh reports of disorder."

And if the evidence around Post Traumatic Growth doesn't convince you that it's good for us to experience some pain from hardships (real science-based evidence rather than false evidence that our thinking and conditioning comes up with), the following evidence around Mind-Body Medicine should further demonstrate how repression affects the body's ability to function well, and the importance of expression over repression.

Mind body medicine

Much evidence has emerged over the past several decades to show the link between mental wellness and physical wellness and how stress and depression with no emotional outlet can negatively impact how our bodies function. Our mask causes us to appear calm externally while, internally, there is turmoil, and this can manifest as a great many disorders: from migraine to irritable bowel syndrome and arthritis.

Yes, our mental state can directly impact our physiological function and health.

Far better to focus on improving our mental wellness, than continuing to repress feelings, which can lead to physical illness. Evidently, you do not need to be afraid of repressed feelings and the sooner you express them the better, because they are making you tired and robbing you of your joy.

Some physical manifestation could be

Your muscles are tense holding them in and hiding them.

Your jaw may be tensing not speaking about them.

You may have psychosomatic symptoms like IBS and headaches, or other symptoms.

Louise Hay who healed herself from cancer and lived to the ripe old age of 90, wrote a multi-million selling book on the mind and body connection and how it can lead to metaphysical disease. In You Can Heal Your Life she listed the various bodily ailments and possible metaphysical causes, along with affirmations to begin healing those ailments.

I am a great believer in mind-body medicine - the link between our mind and body and how we can literally feel our way to freedom and good health. In fact, I wrote a dissertation for my masters on the subject of Irritable Bowel Syndrome. My hypothesis was that repressed anger, frustration and stress were found to be the root cause of IBS and, even though it was a single case study, I had suffered this condition myself. It was only when I learned to express my feelings that I began my recovery. And now you can too!

Since then a lot of my patients have reported that the expression of their irritability and stress has relieved their symptoms.

And yet, despite all the evidence to support the health of our mind impacting the health of our bodies, it is still taboo to talk about mental health compared to physical health. Fortunately, it is becoming more acceptable to talk about it, thanks to campaigns including our very own royal Princes and other people in the public eye, but we're not quite where we should be yet.

Taboo

As a result, I've often wondered why, when someone is physically ill and has a diagnosis, people will empathise with that condition and talk about it, "Oh Jane has got a flare up of her IBS." "Mary is suffering with her blood pressure; it is very high at the moment." "Bob's back is bothering him again."

But no one wants to say "my daughter is suffering from depression or anxiety." Why? Because that diagnosis is perceived as a failing or, perhaps they are afraid that the daughter will go to the therapist who will tell her it is to do with her childhood, and they fear the guilt and blame that comes with that diagnosis.

Remember our friend John? When I asked him how he felt about doctors finding nothing wrong with him physically he replied, "I wish in some ways the medics had found a physical problem."

On first hearing this sounds perverse doesn't it? Why would you want a physical illness to be found? Yet, many people with depression and anxiety would prefer a physical illness for many reasons.

1) It validates their discomfort.

2) Others then validate their struggle.

3) The person has empathy for themselves and doesn't have to feel embarrassed when his friends say "See! There's nothing wrong with you. You've had all the tests so just get on with your life. There's nothing to worry about!"

4) The person doesn't have to admit that their disease comes from a fearful mind and numbed feelings.

As you can see, a lot of this comes from the need for external validation and concern around what other people might think.

Thank goodness a lot of the old messages have lapsed, like sending a daughter away because she was with child out of wedlock, but the subtle messages and fears around 'what will other people think?' remain.

Being addicted or mentally unwell is sometimes still frowned upon in 2019 and it's only recently that mental illness is considered a diagnosable disease or illness.

Conversely, if you are suffering physically, everyone is kind to you. They send you grapes, cards and flowers. The people I have met in my clinic who are psychologically unwell or suffering from addiction, rarely receive this kind of love. In fact, the opposite is true.

Often they are made to feel as if it is all their fault, which makes them feel worse. But what if the alcoholic is self medicating his or her pain but is constantly dismissed as being 'a drunk'. I've spoken to many addicts in my consultancy who are hurt and experiencing pain.

Imagine if we told someone with MS or cancer that it was their fault. That would be wrong, inaccurate and totally unacceptable. I believe the same to be true in relation to blaming people with mental illness as it being their fault.

Jane is born an only child she has two loving parents. She goes to school comes home is allowed to go to her friend's house. There is always food on the table and clean clothes, she tells me I had a great childhood I don't know what is wrong with me why am I depressed. I shouldn't be indulging myself in therapy and the thought of taking medication....

"WHY DON'T I JUST PULL MYSELF TOGETHER?"

This is a common statement my clients make: "I should pull myself together."

Sadly in 2019 people are telling me that they themselves or their families are making others feel bad for not being happy.

But what my clients actually need is treatment and care (and support from the outside world), just as anyone suffering physically would need.

What they don't need is blame, shame or guilt. Because feeling guilty only adds to the pain.

Enforced gratitude and guilt = Guiltitude

I was told as a kid. You have food, shoes and clothes, we live in a nice house, you are not starving like the children in Africa and you have a roof over your head. On hearing this our misery sounds like a 'high class problem' and indeed, socially, it is.

However, it has been reported by the United Nations Sustainable Development Solutions Network that people in some western countries are less happy psychologically than people in some of the poorer countries in the world. Happiness is a complex topic and, as The World Happiness Report discusses, lack of equality and trust in government leaders can mar the happiness levels of those living their lives in third world countries; but the rise of comparison via social media and the day to day stresses of daily life in the western world does greatly impact our level of life satisfaction. Those in poorer countries have disease and other problems to deal with. However, their friends and relatives are not filling their minds with do's and dont's. They live far simpler lives without such overt comparison and striving.

I admit everyone should have their basics and I want to live in a world where that happens.

But the basic we have lost is loving and accepting ourselves. If having basic needs on tap is a reason to tell ourselves we have to conform to other people, it is a high price to pay.

I remember telling my dad once I was 'fed up'.

"Fed up?" he said. There are a lot of people in intensive care who are "fed up".

"Oh," I thought, "that is true. I don't have a right to be fed up."

And yet, all human beings have the right to feel all of their emotions, including feeling fed up, despite having plenty to be grateful for. Gratitude from a place of guilt is not gratitude, it's 'guiltitude'. Feeling grateful because we ought to, doesn't boost our wellbeing as much as genuine gratitude and appreciation for what we have.

I am still glad my father told me that. After all, he had come through a war and holding on to that attitude of gratitude, that we are alive and well and can always find something to be grateful for - well, that's an imperative attitude to have in order to feel satisfied with our lives as they are.

However, the fact is, I was fed up at that moment. That was a real feeling. Probably because I couldn't do my homework or my friend had upset me. I was feeling down because, in my world, something was bothering me. And that's ok. We should allow ourselves to feel bothered, as it's a true feeling that shouldn't be repressed.

As such, it would have been great if he could have said "there are people in intensive care who would love just to be fed up but, come on, let's discuss what you are fed up about."

In that way, he would've nodded to the notion of having a lot less to feel fed up about than some and cultivated an attitude of gratitude within me, but he would also have honoured my feelings, which were real and were felt. Both existed.

The balanced way of thinking and feeling would have helped me to know that sometimes, being fed up was real and there was a way to process it. By honouring our feelings and talking them through, we can process them and figure out solutions to problems or lean in to acceptance for what we can't change. Either way, expression is healthier than repression.

Being in tune with our feelings and, most importantly, giving ourselves PERMISSION to FEEL them, is key to effecting this change.

So right now, I'd like you to do something for me (actually, for you!)

I want you to write yourself a permission slip, to allow yourself to feel your feelings and to express them.

Go on. Write out below what you are permitting yourself to do.

I'll start.

I, Catherine Taylor, give myself permission to be human; to feel my feelings and to express them as best I can.

Your turn.

I,_____, give myself permission to: _____

_____

You see, the problem is that we often think something is wrong with us and that the rest of the world is ok. First we feel out of sorts; sad, fed up, depressed and/or anxious. These are real feelings that EVERYONE feels to certain extents. But, we don't tend to broadcast these feelings as we are all wearing this mask to hide those feelings and paint a picture on social media that everything is awesome, even when it's not.

The fact is, everyone does not have it all together. Everything is not awesome for anyone. Even the most optimistic hopeful people are not happy and joyful all of the time. Why? Because they are human too!

Unfortunately, the feeling that everyone else is fine and there's something wrong with us, makes us believe that it's just how we are; it's down to our personality or something that belongs to us. We may start to think that is just the sort of person that I am 'I am a misery, I am not the life and soul of the party.'

I used to think there was something wrong with me while everyone else was ok too. WHY? Because we are conditioned to believe that everything is awesome for everyone other than us. It's often how the world and our brain works.

But we can stop this treadmill and step off it. We can regain control and see life through a new lens. We can give ourselves permission to release our false expectations and perceptions, to let go of our inaccurate thinking and to get under the hood so we can express our repressed feelings and start to dream and remember who we are, warts and all, and where we want to go.

As we've learned in this and the previous chapter, feeling our feelings, giving ourselves permission to lean into all of our emotions and truly feel, that's the route to freedom and the path back to ourselves. Unfortunately, the tendency is to lean away from our feelings rather than lean in to them. In this way we lean towards numbing rather than nourishing, which leads to languishing rather than flourishing.

Uncovering our truth

Once we have established what does not agree with us we can begin to get in touch with our gut feeling and give ourselves chance to dream again and think about some options of our own.

It is well known that the people in our society who have created music, stories and inventions began dreaming when they were very small. Often the children who were in trouble at school or at home for looking out of the window instead of paying attention to what the teacher was feeding them became quite happy achievers, when all the while they were being told that they would never amount to anything. I love those stories when a successful happy person recounts how they were not academic at school because they were always thinking about writing songs or making furniture or designing clothes or cutting hair.

In spiritual terms it is said that the first step to bringing your dreams to fruition is IMAGINATION.

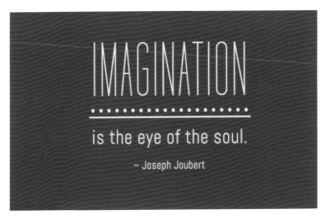

IMAGINATION

is the eye of the soul.

– Joseph Joubert

Many leading thinkers of our time, from Earl Nightingale to Deepak Chopra have explained that what we think about and pay attention to, with 'relentless curiosity', without giving up, we can achieve and become. Texts about the Law of Attraction also suggest that what we think about, we bring about. While Quantum Physicists who study energy are now devoting time to proving it.

So we owe it to ourselves to devote time to dreaming; to thinking about what matters most to us; to question what's getting in our way and to imagine the future of our dreams.

A lot has been written about visualisation and there's a lot to be said about repetition in regard to learning. The more we repeat thoughts about our desired outcomes, the more likely we are to bring about our hearts desires. And the more we practice our skills, the better we become.

Children learning to walk never give up, they just get back up each time they stumble and they keep on going until they are walking. That child was you once. You did that! You have that grit and determination and resilience within you still.

You might think, 'oh no, I'm too old' or 'it's too late for me to learn something new'. But it's never too late.

I recommend finding something you loved to do as a 10 year old or something you've always wanted to try doing, and try something small. It could be learning to play an instrument, joining an exercise class, painting a picture. Across the buffet of joyful activities there will be something for you and if you keep trying something small, you'll find something to suit you.

You can only say you don't like something when you have tried it. If it is something you don't like, you may realise why so and get closer to finding an activity that you would like instead. And who knows what will happen as you become more open to trying new things. Fate may bring you to meet someone at an evening class who introduces you to something you love.

The world truly is your oyster. But only if you show yourself the respect you deserve.

In order to release the shackles of the past and gain hope around the future, as well as leaning in to those feelings and expressing them, it's also important to learn to love yourself, to prioritise taking care of YOU!

"It's not selfish to love yourself, take care of yourself, and make happiness a priority. It's a necessity."

Mandy Hale

CHAPTER 5
Trusting and pleasing yourself

The world is full of myths - the myth that feeling, expressing and releasing your feelings (including pent up pain) will somehow destroy you. When, in actual fact, the truth is that doing so will set you free and enable you to escape from the past and build a great future.

Another myth is that self-care/self-compassion/self-trust/self-love is selfish. When, in actual fact, the opposite is true; focusing inwardly better equips us to focus externally so, when we take care of ourselves and are kind to ourselves, when we trust our intuition and accept ourselves, we become better able to serve others.

You can't pour from an empty cup - so taking care of you is important. Furthermore, you can't love others properly (with compassion) until you love and have compassion for yourself.

Being brave enough to feel your feelings takes time but it is has to be built on a foundation of loving yourself. Courage and bravery are the ingredients that bring FREEDOM and you are worth it, even if you don't believe that yet (because your beliefs have been built on a foundation of self-loathing, formulated from external influences and untrue stories you've accumulated over time).

So, with that in mind, let's think about how we can love ourselves?

Because, let's be honest, loving ourselves is one of the things we were probably told was not ok to do. If you say 'I love myself' out loud, it feels wrong. Loving yourself in this way is frowned upon. But why? It feels awkward in a 'who do I think I am?' kind of way. Our perception of self-love is one of arrogance. It's an insult when we say, 'oh my goodness, he is so in love with himself.' And yes, overt arrogance and superiority is not an attractive or aspirational trait. But that's the kind of self-love where the self-lover positions themselves as more important than anyone else, as superior self-importance.

And yet, you and I are important and our selves should be important to us. Not to the detriment of others, not in a selfish way where we don't consider others or treat others as we wish to be treated, but in a balanced way where we care for our minds and bodies and we speak kindly to ourselves rather than harshly. That kind of self-care, self-love, self-compassion is critical to our wellbeing and, the happier we are, the happier those around us who we wish to serve are.

Yet you and I have been told that loving ourselves is selfish and that other people are more important. Whilst another person is very important, to truly care and empathise with another person it is only possible to be authentic if we love ourselves first. If not we are back to paying lip service, saying what we ought to say, but not really feeling it.

How can I give you anything with authenticity that I don't actually have?

I may want to lend you a £1000 but if I am bankrupt, how can I?

I may want to give you my love and attention but if I am bankrupt of love and attention myself how can I?

And herein is the reason why, if you want to build your emotional bank account so that you are in credit, and therefore able to give love, you need to accrue a decent balance by loving yourself sufficiently.

Depression is like being emotionally drained and bankrupt, but it is also the sign that we have to build a savings account to be a millionaire in love with ourselves.

So now we know what is keeping us bankrupt, how do we start saving up?

By cultivating self-compassion, self-forgiveness, self-acceptance, self-worth and self-trust, is how.

Be a millionaire in love with yourself

YES that's sounds rather grandiose doesn't it?

I make this statement from a deserving stance, rather than a shallow egotistical one.

Someone cleverly pointed out the EGO stands for Edge God Out! Whether you believe in God or not, for me God means love and kindness, non-judgement. We can practice this ourselves by not judging others and being loving and kind to others. Yet, I can't remember ever being taught to be loving and kind to myself, I seem to remember being told that to think of myself was selfish.

No wonder we aren't very well versed or practised in the art of self-compassion.

Of course, that's quite a British way of thinking. In America over the past few decades immense amounts of money have been poured into raising self-esteem because it has been proven that high levels of self-esteem can make you happier and more productive. However, there is a fine line between having healthy high self-esteem and the unhealthy superiority and self-importance which comes from narcissism.

From one extreme to the other, there is another more balanced view on how best to love ourselves, without having to see ourselves as better than everyone else - self-compassion.

Says self-compassion expert, Kristen Neff, "Rather than trying to define our self-worth with judgments and evaluations, what if our positive feelings toward ourselves came from a totally different source? What if they came from our hearts, rather than our minds?"

She goes on to say, "Rather than managing our self-image so that it is always palatable, self-compassion honours the fact that all human beings have both strengths and weaknesses."

Yes, rather than continuously beating ourselves up for our failings, and determining how worthy we are based on our successes and failings, it's far better to see them as "merely part of the process of being alive."

Says Kristen Neff. "Our minds may try to convince us otherwise, but our hearts know that our true value lies in the core experience of being a conscious being who feels and perceives."

In this way, unlike self-esteem or the selfish perception of self-importance, self-compassion isn't dependent on being above average or amazing or on how much we achieve, it's about self-care and embracing the whole spectrum of who we are, including our fragility and flaws.

Forgive yourself!

Something else religion talks about is forgiveness as an important moral code from which to live. However, how many of us believe that we can forgive ourselves? In days gone by and even today, in some religions, it is the job of the priest to tell us we can say something or do something in order to be forgiven. If Jesus or other prophets died so that our sins could be forgiven then why do we berate ourselves so much?

So how do you become a millionaire, in love with yourself? As well as 'feelings' and 'freedom', another big 'f' factor is forgiveness.

Forgiveness of others is important because without forgiveness, it poisons and bankrupts you. Holding grudges and bitterness makes you feel worse than when you let it go. You can't get better if you still feel bitter. If you have done something and you can apologise to the person in person or via another mode of communication, that's all well and good. I know that Alcoholics Anonymous have this as part of their 12 step programme.

Additionally, forgiving yourself releases guilt. So if you have hurt someone because you yourself were hurting, then forgive yourself. Obviously this is a complex idea, because you can't go through life excusing yourself for treating others terribly because you are a victim of hurt yourself. However, if you are committed to working on yourself and ensuring that, from this moment on, you will treat others (and yourself) well, then self-forgiveness can be a wonderful way to lift a weight from your being and to accrue some emotional credit.

By showing yourself love and compassion, you can go from emotional bankruptcy towards having optimum psychological capital reserves. You can go from self-loss to self-love.

We've already explored how important it is to start trusting ourselves, by listening to our gut and changing our thinking to be more flexible and, more importantly, accurate! We've explored how letting the anaesthetic wear off is important, so we can release repression and move towards expression and, in doing so, get our SatNav working again, so we can travel in the direction of our dreams and true purpose.

Now it's time to move from self-dismissal and lack of self-worth to self-care and self-value. In fact, you may find you need to take these steps BEFORE you are ready to express your feelings. And that's ok. It's worth taking whichever step feels right to you.

It may feel like it's a long road to travel from self-hatred and doubt to self-love and confidence, but the route there isn't as arduous as you may believe. Yes, you may have been conditioned to think you aren't good enough, aren't loveable or have minimal value. But the fact is, ALL HUMAN BEINGS are valuable, unique and loveable. We all have it in ourselves to be good enough. But the engines of comparison (social media, magazines and keeping up with the Jones's) have led us to believe that we are not good enough.

The truth is, we are enough and we each have our own value - we each bring something to the world.

As we begin to tune in to our own inner feelings, to truly listen to ourselves, we begin to move from self-doubt and self-comparison to self-trust and self-compassion.

Here's how it works -

STEP ONE - LISTEN TO YOURSELF - you adhere to your gut feeling and make a decision, which is proven to be the right one or you ignore your gut feeling and make a decision, which is proven to be the wrong one. This gives you a body of evidence to support the belief that listening to your gut feeling is worth practising. This also helps you to move from self-doubt to self-trust. Also, tuning in to your own judgements (of yourself and others) about what you DON'T want will lead you to better understand what you DO want.

STEP TWO - LOVE YOURSELF. Secondly, as you start to learn to value yourself, you stop automatically comparing yourself with others and, whenever you do find yourself making those critical judgements and beating yourself up, for whatever reason, you begin to practice giving yourself a break. That's self-compassion and that is the key to accruing emotional credit, so you can pull yourself up and out of the darkness and into the light.

When you give yourself the acceptance and approval you deserve, you become rich.

So let's explore these two steps, one by one.

Listen to yourself

Listen to yourself. You have been listening to others and it hasn't worked!

Once we've removed the anaesthetic, released the conditioning and begun expressing our feelings we begin to find it easier to notice how we feel in our bodies in response to different situations. With practice, we get better at listening to our gut feeling, at tuning into our intuition.

But why is listening to our gut feeling so important?

Well, after a good deal of research, scientists now refer to the gut as the 'second brain'. This is because they've established a strong connection between gut health and mental health.

This connection exists because millions of neurons reside in the tissue lining our gastrointestinal tract (our vagus nerve).

These neurons in our gut actually communicate with our main brain and directly impact our stress levels, emotions, anxiety, decision making and memory. As a result of this interconnectedness, it has even been discovered that, by looking after the balance of gut bacteria, the less intrusive stress is likely to be in our lives.

Furthermore, we can tap into how we 'feel' in our gut to guide us emotionally.

How to tune in to your intuition and listen to your gut?

First, it's important to understand how our decision-making tends to work. We have a rational slower and deliberate system and an older and faster intuitive system. The older system tends to react first to information, hence why it can often feel strange to make a head-over-heart decision, given that our heart or gut has already decided. Sometimes the head is right and sometimes the heart is. But, having the ability to listen to your heart or gut feeling helps equip you with a wider sense of the situation and make a more balanced and more well-informed decision.

In the 1980s, pioneering psychologist, Dr Marsha Linehan created DBT (Dialectical Behavioural Therapy) after discovering that the extreme logic of CBT (Cognitive Behavioural Therapy) made some of her suicidal patients feel invalidated as challenging the belief systems they held, felt like more finger-pointing of their unworthiness and foolishness, rather than as a tool which everyone can use to challenge beliefs we have, which aren't our fault. Whose fault it was that they held these beliefs didn't matter to them, because they'd been conditioned to believe themselves unworthy and foolish. So they, of course, blamed themselves as they'd been conditioned to do, and saw CBT as showing up another thing they hadn't got right.

She developed a concept called Wise Mind to augment the logic of CBT, in order to 'overlap' and find balance between 'Reasonable Mind' and 'Emotion Mind'. Her research had shown that we need both and, in order to tap into the power of both, we need to cultivate a peaceful sense of knowing, a gut feeling which gives us a sense of truth.

We're in our wise mind when we just KNOW something to be

true. For example, if you were asked to explain why cruelty to animals or rape or racism were wrong, you'd be able to write a logical list of the reasons. You'd also be able to feel via your own personal emotional reaction why they are wrong. That middle ground, between feeling why and explaining why results in knowing why, and that is your intuition.

Of course, thanks to FEAR, we may get confused because we fear something rather than know something. That's when CBT and the like do come in to play, because we can explore the False Evidence Appearing Real and collect evidence to the contrary.

Intuition is driven by a sense of knowing. Fear is driven by a sense of uncertainty. Fear is about 'what ifs' and inaccurate thinking. Intuition helps us to know that something is/feels right or wrong. Fear only predicts what COULD go wrong, but it is not based on factual evidence (Reasonable Mind), only on Emotional Mind and only on future worries. It focuses on the worst case scenario rather than the most likely case scenario.

Therapies like CBT and DBT help you figure out the most-likely scenarios and bring more accuracy into play. They focus on now rather than the future - the latter is something we cannot predict.

"This is right or wrong" is what intuition says.

"Oh no, what if this is wrong?" is what fear says.

One of the best ways to tap into your sense of intuition and practice LISTENING TO YOURSELF is to use those calm reflective moments after a crisis or emergency when you are considering and pondering on what happened rather than reacting in the moment to that crisis or emergency. This is when we see and feel and hear most clearly. It's during these reflective post-adversity times that we can best listen to ourselves and cast to memory what that feels like. How do we feel in our bodies? And what is our mind saying?

Another way to tap into what feels right is to pretend a friend is asking you to guide them on the decision you're trying to make. Do you have a feeling about whether or not to proceed with something? Or do you go through the evidence with them and take a more rational logical approach? If you can figure out how they might find their 'Wise Mind' intuition, in the middle of logic and gut feeling, you'll be better equipped to do so yourself.

Another exercise to try is to keep a small notebook in your pocket and, each time you need to make a decision, try to pay attention to how your gut feels. Make a pros and cons list and see how you feel in your gut when you make a decision for or against something. Does one feeling feel different to the other and, if so, can you determine which feels right?

Before we were verbal we communicated to our parent that we required something, be it food, changing or comforting through our feelings. Until the feeling was attended to we probably went on crying out until the transaction was satisfied. Once we became verbal that's when we learned to wait or contain the feeling. Again whilst we cannot live in a world where everything happens in our time and some control of what we want or need has to include the needs of others fully repressing our needs is a recipe for you to feel resentful, hurt and angry.

It is when we want to discover our soul path, our life purpose, or something of more significance in our lives that we must listen to our gut.

And, each time we do so, we are listening to our inner child, we are giving our soul a voice, we are acting like the devoted parent who hears her baby cry and figures out what they need, whether it's food, sleep, a nappy change? Each time you listen to your gut you are figuring out what YOU need and that's vital to living a good life.

For only once you have attended to your needs can you attend to those of others.

Serving others

If you're a nice person, you like to help out friends or family members who need your help. This may have led you towards being a martyr - putting everyone's needs ahead of your own. This can be tiring and emotionally stunting. Indeed, often times, people who are depressed find others a drain on their energy.

They've been so used to soaking other people's ideas up like a sponge that, if others are negative, then the empathic person can soak up the negativity of the person that they are with.

Until now, you may well have listened to others and taken on their beliefs as your own or over-empathised and soaked up all their negative energy. Rather than giving all our love away, we can direct some of it back inward and, in doing so, we'll be better able to love others.

Because we can't love others until we love ourselves. The latter enables us to validate and soothe ourselves rather than seek validation externally. So, in building our self-worth bank account, we can accrue enough love to be better able to give love out.

When you honour listening to yourself, listening to others becomes easier. In fact, everything you give to yourself will be easier for you to give to others. In no way am I suggesting you stop giving to others, just bring some balance between giving to others and giving to yourself.

Fit your own mask first

I used to think that 'fitting your own mask first' as you're told to do in the airplane safety announcements, would be so selfish. Wouldn't it be better to help the children and the old people. No it wouldn't until you are safe yourself, because you can't help as many. You need to make sure you are safe first, before you can offer that safety to others. The rescuer has to be fit. This is why it's so important to get yourself psychologically fit before being of service to others.

Remember how sometimes saying 'good morning' leads to negative feelings which we then hate ourselves for? Can we therefore agree that not loving ourselves leads to an inauthentic way of being in the world? It surely makes better sense to try the win-win exercise of loving ourselves so we may then authentically care for and enjoy another person.

Intimacy

Intimacy, there can be many different meanings and contexts to this word. People mostly associate it with the physical.

Emotional, intellectual or spiritual are all other ways of being intimate.

But I think for the context of this book intimacy has to start with you knowing as much about YOU as possible. An intimacy with yourself.

I call this Into-Me-I-See

Until you really know yourself, how can you possibly bring an unknown you to another human being. You can only bring a false-self or repressed self. This is why so many romantic relationships fall apart because we often project our repression or hurt into the other person and often times vice versa.

This is why we should know ourselves before even entertaining the idea of believing we are really intimate with someone.

So Into-Me-I-see and then hopefully a transparent Into-You-I-see.

What about that for an idea of seeing through the correct lenses.

Love yourself

As explored, loving yourself is not your default way of being. It was when we were born free but ever since then we've been told it's selfish or arrogant. However, you've now learned how important it is to take care of ourselves, be kind to ourselves and listen to ourselves. All of this constitutes self-love. But how do we go about loving ourselves?

Step 1 is self-acceptance and validation. Self-acceptance leads to self-compassion, which leads to self-care. It's important to begin to validate yourself rather than seek validation from others. And yet the latter is our norm. We can still care for others without them controlling us, by seeking their validation. No, we can care for and validate ourselves. In fact, as we've touched on, we need to do so before being able to fully engage in a decent relationship.

Too many romantic relationships fall apart because, once the honeymoon period is over and not enough validation is coming forth, we believe that the person no longer loves us, so the relationship begins to disintegrate. When we accept ourselves, validate ourselves and show ourselves love, respect and compassion, the desperation to feel loved by others is lessened.

That's not to say that we no longer need to feel loved or to feel like we belong, those are human needs which come high up the hierarchy of what humans require. It simply means we are able to find balance without putting all of the need for love under other's control.

Funnily enough when the honeymoon period is in full bloom, we believe we are worth something. In this way, we only seem to love ourselves on condition that the validation from the loved one is available.

Loving ourselves only when validation is coming from others is like being on drugs. We are only happy when we are getting our fix. This 'Fix' kind of 'F' factor, much like 'Fear' does not work. Nor does any other kind of addiction, the root of which comes from needing to feel 'whole' or 'better' or 'enough'

We have to fix our relationship with self-love; that is our mission. Because, once that task is complete most other artificial fixes disappear. Once we love ourselves we feel good enough, because we validate and accept ourselves just the way we are, regardless of external validation. In short, we VALUE ourselves, and that sense of being worth something is vital to living a good life and being free from the inner and external critics which seek to damage that sense of value.

According to statistics, many people who win the lottery have lost it or given it all away in five years. This is an indication at some psychological level that they didn't believe they were worth the fortune and didn't invest it wisely and enjoy themselves. This is tantamount to coming 360 degrees and saying 'I am not really worth it. I don't deserve it. I know my place and it is poor, be it poor in money or poor in worth of any kind.'

Interestingly, researchers have also discovered that lottery winners return to their pre-win level of happiness soon after winning. They've found that circumstances, such as windfalls or setbacks, are less responsible for our happiness than we think. What we feel and what we do - our mindset and the actions we take provides the sustenance for our well-being. This is due to something called the hedonistic treadmill, this feeling of 'I'll be happy when...' and, once we've achieved our goal, we soon return to our pre-goal level of happiness and so strive for the next, 'I'll be happy when...' goal. Hence why gratitude and mindfulness and savouring are all such important ways to sustain our happiness levels as they focus on making the most of now, rather than on what might make us feel better in the future or what we've done in the past. And, in order to make the most of our present, validating who we are and what we have is far better than wishing we weren't us or wishing we had more.

When people sadly ask, *"what is the point in life?"* I answer *"the point is YOU!"*

You have so much potential, so much to be proud of and grateful for and so much to learn and build and grow and experience and live. Each individual does. We were born free and we can return to that freedom. We can have hope - we can even have hope for a better future, but we first need to focus on what is right with us and love ourselves, rather than constantly tell ourselves what is wrong with us and hate ourselves.

Only then can we accumulate value. When we see the value in ourselves. Bankruptcy of your happiness is the worst debt to be in. Imagine getting to the end of your life and realising you had the potential to be a millionaire in love with yourself and your life and you had the power and you didn't love yourself enough to work a little bit to achieve it. I truly hope this book serves as a reminder of how special and unique and VALUABLE and WORTHWHILE you truly are.

Yes, you are worth putting in a bit of effort.

You could be doing a job that you don't like, or be in a relationship that drags you down, but you might be afraid to put the work in to change it. This is happening because you are still not in credit with your value. Once you begin to value yourself, you start to see that it's worth working on the areas of life that you're not happy with. You are worth it!

So let's look at some small ways you can start to build your self-worth bank account.

Self-worth: Celebrate your difference and uniqueness

Everyone is unique and different with different likes, dislikes, hopes, dreams, strengths, weaknesses. A key part of loving ourselves is to see these differences as valuable and to celebrate your difference and uniqueness.

In order to truly care for yourself, it's important to care about your opinions, to care about your passions, to care about your differences; about what makes you, you!

Caring about these things leads to joy and freedom. How? Because we don't give up on our choices, just because our friends and family don't agree. We don't try to convince ourselves that their opinion is better than ours, especially when we truly feel passionate about something.

Science tells us that every snow flake is different. Why then wouldn't every one of us be different? We need difference, otherwise we would all be clones of each other.

In nature the daffodil does not say to the tulip *"hey mate wrong colour"*. The sunflower doesn't say to the daisy. *"Hey shorty."* No, nature accepts and blends and there we find beauty.

Just because we have good results in academic subjects everyone shouldn't tell that person "you are clever you could be a doctor or a scientist". That person may love the outdoors and want to be a fisherman or a stone mason but, once they have been praised for their academia, the SatNav of the person can become confused and start to believe their peers and gives up on what matters most to them.

This losing our love for ourselves and our true path in life starts very early on in life as the trans-generational conditioning leads us to stop making up our own minds, and yet our minds are OURS to make up. Sadly not many people realise this completely until it is too late. So we repress our own wishes to be loved and praised and validated by the people we love so we can be loved. Thus we become estranged from our own self and often don't realise it.

Let's redress the balance and make our own minds up. By placing value on our own desires and hopes and dreams, on what sparks us and excites us and truly matters to us, we can start today and build a better future.

We can now see what has been preventing us from recognising our own value. We know that our value has nothing to do with our material possessions, but in what we bring to the world. As such, material value has to be the icing on the cake, not the cake itself.

Hurt people, hurt people

Only people who are hurting hurt others.

People who are hurting often lash out at others and hurt them. This tends to be more of a cry for help than an intention to hurt - in hurting someone else they are crying out to let someone know how much they hurt. However, often times the person they hurt rejects them and so they conclude that they must be an awful person and so they deserve to be rejected - a self-fulfilling prophecy to themselves that they are mad, bad, sad or all three and the world has rejected them. Yet this is not true - another inaccurate belief fed by this perpetual loop of hurt. The truth is, this person is hurting - they are a victim of someone else's hurt and so it goes on.

Some people turn the pain inward and self-harm to release the pain but they don't deserve that - more pain, on top of the original pain.

If you are still hurting, I suggest that you lean in to the pain, feel and express the hurt, but don't be angry because you believe you deserve to be hurt. Remember this trans-generational programme you've got caught up in, through no fault of your own.

We have the opportunity right now to stop the perpetual loop of hurt people hurting people or hurting themselves further.

We are all victims of victims to some extent. This perspective displays empathy and can spark a deeper sense of forgiveness of others and self-forgiveness too. This forgiveness is another important F-Factor towards freedom.

However, if we repress the pain and only let it out by lashing out, the pain doesn't go away it only gets worse, in a perpetual loop where we are hurt by others, so we hurt others and then turn our hurt on ourselves through self-loathing or self-harm.

Worthlessness and self-loathing

Sadly, other people confirm their own self-judgements such as they tell them, "you are not an ok person to do this" and, so once again, this confirms their worthlessness. They feel great guilt and emotional pain that they anaesthetise their way of choice. Sometimes even gambling in the hope they can return to the fold with some worth. Not their own self-worth, but perhaps they could acquire some personal worth, what a shame this is.

If this is what has happened to you, if you have that belief that others don't see anything in you worth loving then look at this formula that we have been discussing in this book.

Remember, all souls who have value see value in others because it is in themselves. If you compare yourself with others and see everyone as better than you, you are placing value on others, so you see value in others. This means, you must have value yourself. You can't recognise value in others unless there is value in yourself, even if you can't see it yet.

Seeing ourselves as worthless rather than worthy is such a waste of our lives, because every single person has value, ever single life is worthwhile. Let's just take a moment to reflect and wonder: if a person was living a life that was true to them and had empathy and love for themselves, why would they want to hurt another person or hurt themselves? They wouldn't. If they valued themselves, they wouldn't want to hurt themselves or others. They'd want everyone to be free and happy. So, if they did experience pain, they'd want to release it and set it free as soon as possible.

When we are hurt or, even when we're not hurt but are conditioned into believing false assumptions, we can end up thinking we aren't good enough - not a good enough mother, father, friend, sibling, spouse, person. This can lead to thoughts that the people we care about would be better off without us, such is the level of suffering and self-loathing. And yet this could never be true. No matter how much you may have hurt someone and no matter how much pain you have endured, the world is a better place with you in it, because you are unique and you have a life.

All you need to do in order to make the most of that life is to turn it from a LIE into a LIFE with the help of this book - removing Fear, leaning into Feeling and Forgiveness and, consequently, finding Freedom.

But, of course, you cannot do any of the above without first trusting yourself. Once you trust yourself you can give fear a seat in the car and listen to it, but you can keep your trusted self in the driver's seat so that you are in charge of the direction, rather than let fear take the driver's seat. When you trust yourself, you are able to lean into the whole spectrum of feelings, even the darkest ones, because you know they are there for a reason and you can lean in to figuring out what that is, so you can grow and develop and flourish. When you trust yourself you can choose to forgive yourself and others, because you are better able to live your life through a lens of compassion and empathy.

Build self-trust

When we start the journey towards building self-trust, we must first value ourselves and value our voice. We need to remind ourselves that our opinion is worthwhile, it matters.

But how do we trust someone else? The answer is; we don't.

Ok, on first reading that sounds awful, but allow me to explain. When you are young you have to trust the adult who is in charge of caring for you and, if they have let you down this is part of what you are recovering from. When I was a child I spoke as a child and now I am an adult I put the childish things away. Now I am in charge of taking care of myself.

What I'm suggesting is that it's ok to put our trust in others when we are children. We don't have the choice. Even if they are incapable of caring for us, they are all we have and, as children, we don't know how to take care of ourselves. But once we become adults, we need to take some responsibility for our own care and that includes HOW WE RESPOND. As such, I call this our 'response-ability'. It's a combination of being responsible for ourselves and our care, and also being responsible for our responses to hurt, pain, hardships and so on.

On the journey to trusting yourself, you are at the crossroads of a battle to know if someone is trustworthy or not, and whether, these people are worth investing your trust in. However, before you jump to the conclusion that someone is not trustworthy, have a little laugh to yourself because, until you can trust yourself to take care of you, you cannot trust yourself either. So, even though it's a convoluted mirror, your trust is still a reflection of you.

So, once again, how do we trust someone? The answer is, we trust the person until we see a sign that they can't be trusted and then we TRUST OURSELVES to choose what we can do about it. For example, let's say you find out someone has lied to or cheated you, or your boss accuses you of not doing something, yet there had been no discussion and you thought all was well. Perhaps you were giving your loyalty and thought you were getting it back. This is when you shouldn't wonder what is wrong with you, when you should not allow the other person to project all the blame into you.

You're an adult, you know right from wrong and you know who feels worthy of your trust and you know how it feels when someone breaks your trust. You are not responsible for their actions, you are only responsible for HOW YOU RESPOND to their actions; for your response-ability.

Of course, with the workplace example, perhaps on reflection you did make a mistake but it hadn't been openly discussed, so you have a chance to respond well by putting your point across via a grown-up conversation.

However, that is building self-trust. You need to be able to speak up for yourself when needed, to show yourself respect and to heed and hear your own voice and allow it to be heard. Because your voice is worthy of being heard.

Repressed individuals doubt themselves so much, they just want to avoid confrontation, embarrassment and blame. So they are ready to apologise even before they have entered into a conversation. In truth they don't value themselves enough to bother and they don't trust themselves to articulate and be seen and heard. After all, for them it has never been the case before, so why bother now?

Until you can assert yourself, it is tantamount to agreeing with the person telling you that you are wrong. If you don't put your point of view across then the person doing the accusing could be forgiven for thinking you were in the wrong, because you said nothing to defend yourself or to demonstrate the value of your opinion.

Frankly, if you don't value your opinion, why should anybody else?

Clients have told me many times that this has happened to them and, after the event, they have spent a long time going over and over the conversation in their mind, thinking about what they should have said and vow to do it next time. Let's be honest here, we've all done that and will likely continue to do that. We can't possibly respond perfectly every time. And yet, when the anger at the injustice is repressed, the only person who is suffering is you.

When you learn to value yourself and TRUST yourself, expression will follow. That's when life becomes less anxious, you don't have to pre-empt situations because, with value, you will trust yourself to have regard for yourself and the other person and deal with it spontaneously - because you trust in your own response-ability. Of course, as with anything, this takes practice. But each time you voice your opinion well and speak up for yourself, you build the muscle of response-ability, and gain more and more trust in you and your ability to respond well.

Remember we can't change others, we can only change ourselves. Equally, if we get clarity and find our own 20/20 vision, it is harder for others to throw their shadows at us. If two people are in darkness, then it is the blind leading the blind.

I have witnessed that when people really trust themselves they cease to have so many difficulties with confusion and mistrust. When their own vision is clear, their SatNav is on target and other people sense it. Other peoples' lack of trust in themselves no longer becomes a problem for you. When you love, respect and trust yourself, you are well on the road to becoming worth a million dollars in your own right.

The best way to trust yourself is to start building evidence that your beliefs are factually accurate and worth believing in. You can only do that when you learn some thinking tools and learn to look at life through the right lens.

So, about that...

BE
YOURSELF
EVERYONE
ELSE IS
ALREADY
TAKEN

Oscar Wilde

CHAPTER 6
Seeing the world through the correct lens

In Chapter 3 we talked about how our thoughts are often inaccurate, based on years of trans-generational conditioning and conditioning from other directors of our story (society/peers/media). We explored how these thoughts, once repeated over time, become firm beliefs which influence our actions and reactions and thus interfere with how we live our lives. Consequently, these thoughts influence the lens through which we see the world. And yet they're not always accurate, so what can we do about that?

The obvious answer would be to ignore those thoughts that aren't accurate and only believe the ones that are true. But that's not how our minds work. As we have learned, thoughts are neurons firing and, the more we repeat those thoughts, the more the neurons fire together, wire together and become neural pathways, which become our beliefs.

And, thanks to our attention bias, it's impossible to 'not think' about something that we're thinking about. We know that trying to push a negative thought away is akin to pushing a beach ball under water, it will simply resurface. As such, the only way to really deal with a negative thought is to pop the beach ball by re-framing any inaccurate thoughts and replacing them with accurate ones, which enable us rather than disable us.

Given how much weight we give to our thoughts and how much impact they have on our lives, surely it makes sense for us to verify their accuracy and, if inaccurate, replace them?

Now, at this point, it's important to remember the difference between a negative THOUGHT and a negative FEELING or emotion. The latter is best leant into and felt, expressed rather than repressed. Conversely negative thoughts can be re-framed.

Lifting yourself out of depression and anxiety and towards a happier life is not all about positive thinking, it's about accuracy.

Until this point, false evidence and false expectations have likely been controlling your life. As such, you could be viewing the world through 'convoluted spectacles'.

Convoluted spectacles

What do I mean by this statement?

I mean that, sometimes, whatever we were programmed with in childhood remains in place, whoever we are relating to.

For example, let's say we have come from a family who have controlled us in some way and repeatedly rejected our opinion. Every time we relate to a new person we expect our opinion to be rejected, we expect the other person not to agree with us, to have a better idea. Such conditioning means we may not even notice how quickly we give up on our own ideas. Yet, as a result of this conditioning, we no longer trust ourselves. And all because of false expectations we've learned and repeated over time.

So we give up our voice and our belief becomes one based on repeated judgemental thoughts that say, 'nobody listens, so perhaps nothing I say is worth listening to' or 'perhaps I am stupid like they always said I was?'

In accordance with these judgements, which have now become our own self-judgements, we see the world through the eyes of those who put those thoughts into our heads. And, each time we find ourselves in a situation where we have the opportunity to voice our opinion and share our ideas, we choose to stay quiet for fear of rejection.

In this way we are living our lives through the lens of other people.

Other times, once we are grown and relating to a partner, friend, work colleague or boss, we might find ourselves automatically feeling defensive, as though the person is not going to agree with us, even before they've opened their mouths. We assume they won't agree, seeing as our past stories tell us that nobody listens to our opinion or agrees with it. So, the minute they say or do something alternative to our opinion, we become stressed and anxious and recoil in a defensive default, before deciding not to share our ideas anymore. We grow fearful of discussion because, for us, it's deemed as conflict and we'd rather choose silence, so we do.

The result of this conditioned response is that people who are genuinely less capable than you may overtake you at work. If you stay silent your great ideas stay silent and nobody benefits from your brilliance. This may lead to a feeling of bitterness, jealousy and resentment - all valid feelings, but they've been brought about because a thought ('who am I to share my ideas? Nobody listens to me anyway. Nobody wants to hear my ideas') becomes a belief and the consequence of that belief is to stay silent.

Deep down, repressed people may feel like they perhaps do have more to offer than they openly give, but fear stops them (because that's what fear does; indeed that's all fear does).

In relationships we often see one person ruling the roost and ignoring their more easy-going partner. The confident one begins to expect the easy going one to do their bidding, and the easy going one just gives up. Yet this is another lose/lose situation, because the controlling partner is fearful of losing their partner's compliance and the compliant partner avoids confrontation and gives up their voice entirely. Nobody wins here.

As these examples suggest, we continue looking through the old lenses of childhood. But when we don't have the right prescription in our spectacles, we can't see properly.

The blind lead the blind

Consequently, we are living our lives BLINDED by our perception of what others might think, blinded by the need for external approval, blinded by the stories we repeatedly tell ourselves based on our early experiences and based on other people's conditioning (which is likely also based on inaccurate assumptions). And yet, these stories are old and out of date and we have the power to rewrite them based on our own internal truth.

When we look through convoluted lenses, we can only see ourselves as the person we think others have wanted us to be; through their eyes, not ours; the way people from our past wanted to see us. And yet, children grow up, humans change all the time. But, when we see the world through convoluted spectacles, the only way we feel comfortable in changing is to create a false self that others will approve of, a false self that lives up to other people's false expectations.

We blend in with our surroundings and behave in ways that we perceive others want us to behave. We become chameleons.

Trying to see what the other person wants or thinking you have to see the world through the old parental or conditioned glasses assumes that we all see the world in the same way.

- But we don't.

- We are all unique.

- We don't all have the same prescription.

So we ought to question our thoughts and beliefs. In doing so, we can get to know ourselves better - our true selves. Rather than base our beliefs and actions/reactions on seeing life through other peoples' spectacles.

We see the world through other peoples' spectacles whenever we seek validation from others yet, in doing so, we grow further and further away from our true selves.

Clear vision and self-validation - know and approve of yourself

Here's an important truth: the person who needs to validate us is us! Nobody else. Indeed, seeing yourself with fresh eyes, through your own prescription lens, is the only way to give you 20/20 vision on your own life.

And 20/20 vision equals clarity!

Gaining clarity is the first step towards finding your way back to yourself; to finding your way home.

As we grow, it's critical for us to keep testing our own vision of ourselves, to question our thoughts and beliefs and be honest with ourselves. We need to test our ideas out, discuss them with others, perhaps find a therapist if you feel like you have nobody to discuss your thoughts and ideas with.

It's worth doing this work, because this is *your* life. It's such a shame to waste it, to let fear lead the way, to live your life through convoluted lenses, because there is real magic in getting clear 20/20 vision on your life.

Life is a mirror

How you see yourself is important for two reasons.

1. Because when you see yourself for who you truly are with true clarity, you become better able at validating yourself, without needing so much external validation and living your life in a way that suits everyone else rather than in a way that suits you. It's YOUR life, so you deserve to live it YOUR way.
2. Like attracts like. Life is a mirror. It can only reflect back to you what you think you are. As the Tao says, "You are what you think you are, if you think you are a failure, you are right. If you think you are a success you are right." Whether you buy into the Law of Attraction or not, our beliefs can have a habit of becoming self-fulfilling prophecies, so it's in our best-interests to think well of ourselves. For most of us, thanks to our in-built negativity bias, that's not the way we're wired, but we have the ability to shift the way we think and to reflect the good. It just takes practice.

Inviting change

It's so fascinating to me that so many clients come to therapy and tell me their partner wouldn't like it if they changed this or that about themselves. They tell me they don't want to rock the boat. In fact, they're scared to. We work on what the fear is based on and then, when they do eventually take a risk and do something they didn't before (at first the partner blames the therapist hahaha, but no, something does change in the relationship, but it's always a positive shift) eventually the partner starts to respect my client more.

When my client feeds back to me and says, "My partner respects me more now and takes me seriously." I say "oh, are they going to therapy as well?" "No," they say. "I've changed."

The partner has changed their response to them because my client has changed.

The moral here is that you can't change someone else; you can't wait for them to accept and value you. The only way you can change someone else's response to you is to change yourself; to do the work on yourself! Only then can the world reflect it back to you.

Only when you put on your new lenses are you able see yourself as you really are. And that's when you begin to earn the respect you deserve, as others start to see that too.

Change starts with a small step.

And you can take a small step today. Even if you just try out one of the tools included in this Chapter, you'll start to shift how you see yourself, how you view your fears and replace thoughts that don't serve you, so that you can break free from the shackles of what's holding you back.

First, let's make list of all the things that are holding you back

Is it:

- Being a people pleaser?

- Feeling unable to say no?
- Fear of being rejected?
- Fear of failure?
- Feeling disloyal to the family, because your family does things differently?
- Hating to disappoint someone else?

Let's take the above a little further to uncover why you might think that way:

- Being a people pleaser? *Why? Because... Pleasing others makes me a nice person.*
  Feeling unable to say no? Why? Because... Saying yes to others ensures I have and keep my friends.
- Fear of being rejected? *Why? Because... Being rejected will leave me lonely and ashamed.*
- Fear of failure? *Why? Because... If people see me as a failure, I will be ashamed and they'll lose respect for me and treat me less well.*
- Feeling disloyal to the family, because your family does things differently? *Why? Because... My family mean the world to me and will be disappointed if I don't do what they think is best for me.*
- Hating to disappoint someone else? *Why? Because... I can't bear to see the disappointment on my Mother or Father's face.*

Ok, so let's get curious about these beliefs and consider another way at looking at them, which may be nearer the truth:

- Being a people pleaser? *Pleasing others makes others believe I am a nice person but, underneath, I resent it. I don't feel nice and I am not happy, I am repressing my true self. (Furthermore, should others want you to be unhappy to please them? If so are others caring about you?)*
- Feeling unable to say no? *Do you want friends who control your life? Do your friends even know that you*

are saying yes when you mean no? Real friends would not want you to do that. Is all this idea of losing friends coming from them or from a conditioning where your family always pressured you into saying yes, or told you that you had disappointed them? Hmmmm. Interesting.

- Fear of being rejected? *If you are rejected because you have pleased yourself then again, what choice: repression or expression?*

- Fear of failure. *Remember the greats have become great on the back of their failings. What if the people you fear won't respect you, do respect you for actually trying? They wish they had the courage to try.*

- Feeling disloyal to the family, because your family does things differently? *If your family wants what's best for you that will include the way that feels right for you, the way that feels most aligned with you as an individual? As such, what if they respect and admire your decision after all? And wouldn't they rather you follow your truth rather than conform to a way that doesn't suit you?*

- Hating to disappoint someone else? *Have you spoken with them? What if they'd be more disappointed that you didn't follow your true path because of your fear of disappointing them?*

These are just a few of the things that may worry you and, as you can see, if you consider other ways of looking at those concerns that hold you back, you can counter them with alternative ways of looking at them.

Make a list of your own.

Consider them.

Check out with your friends and express some of your new thoughts and ideas, especially with the people in your life who perhaps know you are not happy.

As this example illustrates, if you don't have the right prescription, the right lens, you can't see the world or yourself in a clear and accurate fashion.

So let's explore in more detail how to dispute and reframe the thinking that has been holding you back for so long.

Have a debate with yourself

Debating with ourselves is the premise of Cognitive Behavioural Therapy using the Cognitive ABC Model.

This takes an adverse event (A) our beliefs (B) and the actions we take as a result of having that belief (i.e. the consequences) (C) and tweaks the belief in order to generate more accurate and suitable responses.

For example, say you don't get a management job you've applied for. That's the adversity (A); the negative event or circumstance you are facing.

So, let's say your belief (B) is based on a pessimistic explanatory style, and blames the fact you weren't selected for the role on your belief that you aren't skilled enough and are never going to be any good at management. The consequence (C) based on that belief (B) might be to feel sad and disappointed and consequently give up applying for managerial roles, because you feel like there's no point.

A more optimistic explanatory style would believe (B) that you didn't get selected for this specific role this time, because you haven't got enough experience in that industry. As such, you'd conclude, if you did some voluntary work in that industry, you'd have a better chance of being selected for a role for that company in the future. Consequently, rather than give up applying for managerial roles altogether, (C) you'd find ways to gain more experience in the industry you're keen to get into. I'm sure you'll agree, when you tweak your belief in this way you can create a better outcome and become open to wider possibilities.

By getting to know how we think in relation to what happens to us, we can tune into our mind-chatter. This helps us to separate fact from fiction. Then, once you have a better understanding of this internal mind chatter and the consequences on your behaviour, you'll be better able to reconsider and reframe your thoughts to create a better response and outcome.

So, in this example, you'd be able to go from feeling disappointed and giving up applying for management jobs altogether, to feeling determined to gain experience.

Flick the switch back to rational thinking

First, to think rationally, it's important to be calm. When we feel stressed, anxious or worried, the brain switches automatically to the fight or flight response. When it does this, we no longer have access to our rational side of the brain (the pre-frontal cortex) as the emotional side of the brain (the amygdala) seizes control.

The most effective way to get calm is to BREATHE SLOWLY. Other methods include counting backwards by difficult numbers from 100 (say counting back by 7 or 8) and switching your focus to your senses.

This process calms you down so you can talk back to your mind chatter in real time. However, before you can do that, you need to tune in to what your mind is actually thinking and believing.

Take your thoughts to court

In order to effectively validate our thoughts, we need to play detective and collect evidence to dispute our negative thoughts and beliefs. By fact-checking and 'taking thoughts to court', you can find evidence to counter the false evidence you base all of your fears (and many beliefs) on.

That's what we do when we get into a debate with others. If someone suggests that we've done something we didn't do, i.e. they have an inaccurate thought about us and they throw the blame at us, we probably have no problem coming up with evidence to counter their view point, to dispute their claims and prove that they are wrong. However, when it comes to our own self-criticisms and judgements and negative thoughts, we rarely dispute them, even when they are false.

Talking back to your thoughts in a way that challenges them is called re-framing and it comes in particularly handy when re-framing judgemental thoughts and anxious thoughts.

To do this you need to access your own internal mind chatter so you can get to know which thinking traps you tend to fall into. Notice the language your internal radio station plays: For example, you might judge yourself or jump to conclusions with the following prefixes: 'I'm so/such a...', 'I always....', 'They think I'm...', 'He's always', 'I should...'.

Once we get to know the language we to use and the thinking traps we tend to fall into (see Chapter 3) we can start to use the relevant antidotes and begin to consider alternative ways of seeing.

For example, you might assume a friend doesn't care about you if they don't reply to a long message you've sent them. Yet, if you look for the evidence to support or refute that belief, you would likely discover they do care after all. You may remember they work on Wednesdays or perhaps their phone is out of battery. Because, when you reflect back on your interactions with this person, including their most recent reply to another message, you'll recollect many times when they've devoted ample time to comforting, supporting and encouraging you.

By devoting time to taking your thoughts to court, you can find the truth. So the radio station playing 'fake news' can be replaced by tuning in to a radio station which plays more accurate and supportive messages.

When you take your thoughts to court, if you are able to find even a tiny piece of evidence to dispute your thoughts, it means the thought is sufficiently inaccurate to warrant a re-frame.

For example, when Sheryl Sandberg, COO of Facebook and author of *Option B*, lost her husband, she believed her children would never be able to have a happy childhood.

However, she took those assuming thoughts to court and sought evidence to dispute that belief, by speaking with many people who'd lost parents at a young age. In doing so, she was able to prove that false prediction wrong. She found everyone she spoke to had gone on to have happy childhoods and were now well-balanced adults. So she replaced her negative assumed (and inaccurate) thoughts with the factual (and accurate) thoughts to shift her belief and help her and her children journey towards healing.

Once you've replaced an inaccurate thought with a more accurate one, you can evaluate whether it passes the gut test to ensure you're not replacing a wildly inaccurate negative statement with a wildly inaccurate positive statement. For example, if your judgement was 'I'm terrible at painting' and you replaced that belief with 'I'm the best artist in my town,' they would both be inaccurate. A more valid re-frame would be, 'Painting isn't one of my strengths, but I'm improving with practice.'

Accurate thinking

Let's say you're struggling to find a job. (A) You may believe you have nothing to offer and attribute your lack of skills as the reason why you've been struggling. (B). The consequence of that (C) is that you lower your expectations, apply for jobs you're over-qualified for or stop applying for roles altogether.

However, there may be many other reasons why it's not been easy to source work. When you jot those down and assign a percentage to them, you'll be able to see your initial belief that you have nothing to offer is not to blame.

- The economy is pretty slow. 10%
- I've only been looking for a few weeks. 20%
- I'm not applying for roles I'm best matched for as I don't have complete clarity on what I want to do or on what

relevant experience I've brought to previous roles. 60%
- I have nothing to offer and am not skilled enough 10%

As well as demonstrating the inaccuracy of your assumption about the adversity, this process helps figure out a better action to take. In this instance, what could you do to gain more clarity about your relevant experience and what you want to do for a job? Perhaps you could write down everything you achieved in past roles, speak to former colleagues, make a list of the tasks you most enjoy and recollect what you loved to do as a child and whether you might find a job including tasks you enjoy and are good at?

Tackling worries

So far, we've been exploring what to do with our judgemental thoughts. But what about our anxious thoughts, which relate more to what we think *might* happen, rather than to what we think about ourselves, other people or a current situation we're facing.

What tends to happen with our anxious thoughts (also known as our worries) is that they can start off small and of no real consequence and spiral and build into thoughts which can strongly impact our lives, causing stress and anxiety and preventing us from living our lives well.

We start off worrying about what might happen if we fail at something and soon, before we know it, we've had small incremental what if thoughts that have layered upon each other until we've gone from a tiny possible problem to a terrible fear. This is known as 'snowball thinking' as the thought process gathers pace and becomes a great big snowball knocking all other thoughts (and rationale) out of its way as it rolls down hill.

And because our brain doesn't go from the tiny possible problem directly to the huge fear, but instead incrementally builds from one thought to the next, we are tricked into thinking these big scary worries are actually perfectly reasonable and rational, when they aren't. They are False Evidence Appearing Real. How do I know this to be true? Because we can't know exactly what will happen to us in the future. What if worries trick us into thinking that we do, but we cannot predict with accuracy exactly what will happen.

So what can we do about this? How can we stop the snowball and prevent our brains from catastrophising?

We can put things into perspective.

Putting things into perspective

First, we can remind ourselves that we will handle whatever it is we're worrying about and list all the times we've coped in the past. We can also designate some worry time during which we'll explore the possibilities we're worrying about. This gives our fear a voice and a chance to be heard.

Then, if we're still concerned, we can check the facts of the situation. Often times when we bring our thoughts back to fact-checking, we can remind ourselves of what has actually happened rather than imagining all the worst-case-scenarios.

Talking of which, thinking of what the worst-case-scenario might be can be made into a bit of a game. If you imagine the worst possible outcome and then the equally unrealistic best possible outcome, you can attribute a likelihood percentage of those two extreme outcomes happening and then consider the most likely case scenario and again attribute a percentage to that likelihood.

This cognitive tool helps pull ourselves out of a downward spiral and focus on the most realistic outcome. It's a great (and sometimes fun) way to get everything into perspective and bring accuracy and flexibility into play.

For example, let's say you're worried about losing your job.

Worst case scenario would be - lose job, be unable to pay the bills, home repossessed, homeless. (10%)

Best case scenario would be - get a promotion, earn more money than you ever dreamed possible, buy a mansion. (10%)

Most likely scenario would be - put in extra effort to impress your boss, keep job and continue as you were with a greater appreciation for your job. (And, even if you did lose your job, the most likely scenario would be that you'd soon find another one and, in the meantime, contact the bill providers to work out a repayment scheme that works for you in the interim). (80%)

Stay calm, patient and positive and you'll see that worry won't make whatever you're worrying about better, but how you frame your thinking and respond to worrying thoughts will help you gain perspective and stay in a stronger, more resilient frame of mind.

The added value of using this perspective-gaining strategy to generate more accurate thinking and solve problems is that it helps us to recognise how unrealistic our Worst Case Scenario thinking is. What's more, having fun coming up with ridiculous Best Case Scenarios pulls us out of downward spirals and into more positive upward spiral emotions, which broadens our problem-solving ability.

Now, once we've got curious about which thoughts are inaccurate, we can then replace those thoughts with more accurate ones.

We can talk back to our thoughts by saying, 'that's not true, because....' and suggesting 'another way of seeing this is...'. And, once we've gained perspective during the process of worrying, we can suggest a more likely outcome to ourselves.

Getting curious about our thoughts, questioning, disputing and talking back to them helps us develop more flexible and accurate thinking processes, shift our belief system towards something which is more helpful and increases positive emotions. The result is boosted well-being and improved resilience.

Of course, this takes practice, but the reward is freedom. As we begin to question and debate our thoughts and cultivate our own curiosity, we get to know ourselves better and, as we increase our awareness, we become better at seeing through the 'false evidence' that our fears come up with to stop us from living our best lives.

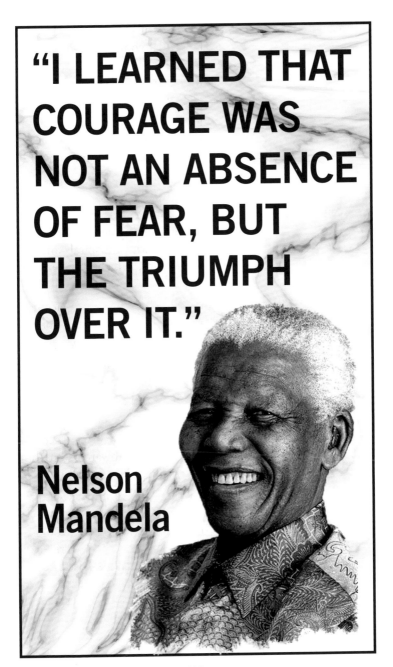

"I LEARNED THAT COURAGE WAS NOT AN ABSENCE OF FEAR, BUT THE TRIUMPH OVER IT."

Nelson Mandela

CHAPTER 7
Replacing F for FEAR
with F for FREEDOM

People fear change. And uncertainty. And failure. Oooh, how people fear failure. But why?

It's time to break down exactly what we are scared of. Only then can we tackle our fears and replace them with freedom. Because knowledge is freedom.

So let's give fear a seat at our committee meeting table. Let's hear what fear has to say?

The committee meeting - hear your fear

Imagine your emotions are committee members in the committee meeting that goes on in your head each day. The chairperson stands up and asks Fear to explain:

'So why is failure so scary for you, Fear? What's up with that?'

Consider fear's reply:

'I'm scared of failing because... it matters to me what others think of me and, if people find out that I've failed, they'll think less of me. I don't want people to think less of me, I want people to respect me, to think well of me, to think I'm great!'

"Ok," says the Chairperson.

"But what if they think you're awesome and brave anyway - because you TRIED?" asks the Chair. "What if they already admire you because you had the courage to try something, regardless of the outcome? What if they're thinking, 'well at least you had the guts to do it, that's admirable, I could never do that, I'm useless.'

Because, guess what... most people aren't thinking much about you - all they care about is what you think of them! In fact, they are most likely comparing themselves to you in a way that you couldn't possibly understand - because they are comparing all your positive qualities and attributes (such as you trying) with all their negative attributes (such as them never feeling brave enough to try).

"But some people will think I'm an idiot. They'll think, 'well that serves you right for taking that risk, you wouldn't catch me doing that,' replies Fear.

"Hmmm, interesting," says the Chairperson. "You're right. Some people might think that, but that's an assumption (because you can't know exactly what every individual will think) and, if they do, it says more about them and their own fears, insecurities and envy, and their need to feel superior, than it does about you and your choices."

"And besides," adds the Chairperson. "You can never please all of the people all of the time. And they'll soon move on to judging someone else based on their own fears and insecurities. But mostly, they'll devote 80 per cent of their time judging themselves."

Hearing our fears can help our conditioned selves consider alternatives and to get to the bottom of why we might be fearful.

"Until you cross the bridge of your insecurities, you can't begin to explore your possibilities," Tim Fargo

What other people might think?

In this case our fear of failure is driven by a deeper-seated fear about what other people think of us. Indeed, many of our fears are - fear of rejection, disapproval, criticism, failure.

As humans we care *deeply* about what others think of us.

This is because of our ingrained survival instinct. Early humans needed to be included to avoid getting left behind. What others thought of us therefore mattered. That's why we've become so conditioned by other people; that's why we've handed over the reigns for fear of other people's reaction to being our true selves. And so we conform and we let fear steer the meeting, rather than be a committee member. We let Fear become the Chairperson, rather than Reason. And, as we know, once we hand over control to Fear (who controls our Fight or Flight Response), our rational reasonable brain cannot function. So Reason gets demoted and goes unheard.

These days, rather than being driven by our need for survival, what others think of us is driven by our social desires. We need to feel accepted and fear not being so.

Yet, when we become focused on external perceptions of us, we can lose sight of who we are. Our essential nature, our internal truth gets lost amid assumptions (of perceptions); our judgement becomes clouded.

The masked false ego-led version of ourselves is desperate for approval to counter all the negative self-talk it receives. This need is also driven by our fear of rejection, which stems from our fear of not being 'good enough'; of being 'less than'.

This spiral is brutal.

Yet we disapprove of ourselves frequently. It's par for the course in human nature, because it's human to judge. But how's that actually working out for us? Considering that we've been consistently disapproving of ourselves for most of our lives, perhaps it's time to start approving of ourselves instead?

The freedom of being enough

Perhaps it's time to start accepting ourselves as good enough? To stop looking for external validation and validate our true essential nature as all that we need?

How about that?

What if all we are is all we need to be? What if we're enough?

We are already fully us, just the way we are. There is only one you and only one me, and that's good enough. We don't need other peoples' judgments, because they don't know our whole story so cannot judge accurately, just as we cannot judge others accurately, because we never know their full story either.

This realisation, that we are enough, just the way we are, is freeing.

Because, when we grasp that it doesn't REALLY matter what other people think of us anymore, it means there is nothing to fear.

Ok, we may still fear rejection but, when we know that we are enough, rejection matters less. When we are able to validate ourselves, external validation matters less and other peoples' perceptions of us matter less.

This is helpful because we can't please everyone all of the time.

The more we remember that fact, the better we become at shifting our fear of what others might think towards our own internal values. We can't please everyone else, but we can please ourselves. However, the only way to do that is to know and truly understand what matters most to us; to tune into our feelings, to gain more clarity on what scares us so we can decide whether that's due to conditioning or nature or down to us?

Fear of feeling

What else do we fear?

You might fear the pain of having your feelings hurt?

You might fear exposing the real you? In case people don't like him or her?

You might fear not being approved of, accepted, loved?

You might fear social embarrassment or exclusion, loneliness?

Most of these fears are driven by the deeper concern around what others think of us; but some are driven by a fear of feeling.

We don't want to feel hurt, to feel pain, to feel sadness. And yet, as we've explored at length in this book, these feelings are valid and important - they show us what matters to us. They serve as indicators and can be catalysts for change and, they can just be part of the whole spectrum of what it means to be human. Either way, it's better to feel them than repress them. We know that now.

As such, we needn't fear feeling hurt, because we have it within us to heal, just as we have it within us to feel all the feelings and move through and onward and upward - towards freedom.

What's stopping you?

We fear failure because we don't want to be perceived as a failure and also we fear what comes with failure - i.e. loss. If our business fails, we might end up being unable to pay our bills, and, worst case scenario worries creep in, we might lose our home.

So FEAR STOPS US from trying. But remember, mistakes are useful learning tools and failure is a step in the right direction, contrary to popular belief. It is far better to try and fail than never bother trying.

Some of the world's biggest stories of failure became success stories, BECAUSE they failed first.

Steve Jobs would never have created all that he did if he hadn't got fired from his own company.

"I didn't see it then, but it turned out that getting fired from Apple was the best thing that could have ever happened to me," said Steve in 2005.

Getting fired showed him what mattered most to him; it proved to him that his passion for his work mattered more to him than the disappointment of failure. So he got on with his next venture, (the aptly titled NeXT) and Pixar and was finally invited back to take on the CEO role at Apple.

"Failure is simply the opportunity to begin again, this time more intelligently," Henry Ford

As such, failure is an OPPORTUNITY. It's a RESET BUTTON. It's not the end! It's a new beginning.

Not only did JK Rowling face rejection after rejection as she submitted her Harry Potter manuscript to various publishers, she told Harvard graduates how she had "failed on an epic scale... an exceptionally short-lived marriage had imploded, she was jobless, a lone parent, and as poor as it is possible to be in modern Britain, without being homeless." Her fears had been realised. And yet she kept on keeping on and the rest, as they say, is history. Rejection gave her more determination to succeed and succeed she did.

> *"Success is failure in progress,"* Albert Einstein

The same is true with change. We fear losing what we have now through change. We fear that people might not like the changed version of us. We fear that we might not like the new life we've created. So, once again, FEAR STOPS US from changing.

Of course, change isn't easy. In fact, change is hard work. And yet, the price for no change could be high if it means you only live half a life. With that in mind, surely change is worth the hardship; worth the effort, because it sets you free.

When we admit to ourselves what we're afraid of, we can feel the fear and move through it. We get to choose whether we let fear STOP AND DISABLE us or whether we let fear SHOW US what matters to us and ENABLE us.

Feel the fear and do it anyway

Now that we understand a little more about what we fear, why we fear it and where those fears come from, let's explore the whole notion of fear itself.

Notice how, at the start of this chapter, we gave fear a seat at the table in our committee meeting. It's important to do so because fear is a feeling and, although it is often False Evidence Appearing Real, it can also be driven by very real feelings, drivers and human needs, such as those explored so far in this chapter. These are valid needs. When we explore them we can give our fears less weight, because once we accept that the fear is driven by a human need to feel like we belong and are accepted and significant, we can do what we can to work with what we have; to cultivate our 'enoughness'.

In this way we do what Susan Jeffers suggests, we 'feel the fear and do it anyway.'

We can't escape fear permanently, nor should we try to. Fear, like worry, can be useful when our life is in danger. Fear stops us from walking home by ourselves through a rough part of town and stops us from taking dangerous risks.

So trying to become fearless could be asking for too much. Instead, we can embrace our fears; feel them and get to know them and then get on with doing the stuff that scares us.

And therein lies the key lesson around fear. Fear is fine as long as we don't let fear stop us from doing something important.

- When fear stops us from taking a risk by starting our own business, that's disabling.

- When fear stops us from going to a new evening class, that's disabling.

- When fear stops us from trying, that's disabling.

And the fear which stops us from trying is conditioned. Like a computer, we've been programmed from our early years without our permission or, rather without ever being in a position to realise it. Before that conditioning we would try and try over and over again.

As children, we're great at learning, because we're not yet afraid to fail. While we are easy to influence, we don't tend to give up easily as we try to walk. Each time we fall down, we just get back up again and, each time we do so, onlookers clap their hands in delight. Every time we form a word, the onlooker claps in delight even if the word is not quite pronounced correctly. Back then, when we are learning, it's a given that we are allowed to get it wrong; we're allowed to make mistakes, and we learn from them over and over again and we persist until we get it right - and so we go from crawling along on our knees to pulling ourselves up, to walking, to running.

That's when the fun begins for parents as their terrible two year old seeks to explore far and wide with no fear. Thankfully, they want the parent's approval, so they seek permission, and, in doing so, they discover boundaries.

This is sometimes where it can go wrong as parents strive to get the balance between allowing a child to try it their way and making sure they are safe. Freedom vs security is a challenge for even the best parent.

By the time we reach the age of four or five, we tend to know our boundaries and will know the importance of staying safe and being kind to others. We'll have learned a little about balance.

Finding balance

And balance is fear's enemy.

Balance finds the middle ground. Balance reigns in fear and balance has your best interests at heart. As such, balance is enabling. Finding balance is our way out from a life ensnared by fear. Balance leads to freedom. Fear keeps us stuck.

I believe balance is the best word in language. It applies to everything we've learned so far. Far better to apply balance to all things than veer towards the extremities.

You might think that love is a better word, but even that has to be in balance. Tough love and kind love; there is a place for both.

Equally, when we make a change in our lives or a change in our mindset, the change has to be in balance. Nature is always searching for balance and so should we. So when we change, we should do so in a way that brings a win/win to the table.

- Taking care of yourself and others, in balance.

- 'Feeling your fears' in balance with 'doing it anyway'.

- Taking the rough with the smooth.

- Balancing appreciation for what we have now with striving for what we hope to have in the future.

- Considering pros and cons and deciding 'on balance' what to do next.

- Finding a happy medium between pleasing yourself and pleasing others.

Finding balance of worth and value, between the extremes of the scarcity mentality vs the arrogant mentality by having the confidence and knowing you are valuable and unique, but staying humble and kind.

And, crucially, finding balance between give and take. If you feel like you have nothing to give yourself, so cannot give to others, try giving people a compliment, a smile, your presence, your time. And as you sew, so shall you reap.

And as you try, so shall you achieve (and fail, but that's ok, because that's how you achieve next time)!

"It takes courage to grow up and turn out to be who you really are"

E E Cummings

CHAPTER 8
Who's life is it anyway?

Taking back the pen to write your own story

As we approach the end of this book, it's time for you, dear reader, to get back in the Director's Chair of YOUR own life and rewrite your own story.

You have it within you to achieve personal mental mastery and control.

You have it within you to take back 'response-ability', to relinquish blame and take ownership of all the experiences in your life.

You have it within you to release the past, so you may unlock the future.

You have it within you to focus on the present, so you may uncover what matters most in shaping what happens next, so you may look forward and achieve your full potential.

We've talked a great deal in this book about the freedom you are born with and how, overtime, we learn to disapprove of ourselves; to accept other peoples' version of the truth and to repress who we are and how we feel. But now, as I hope you've learned the way back home to yourself (and will continue to learn throughout this final chapter) it's time for you to seize control of your story.

In that sense, it's time for a kind of rebirth.

Your mother gave birth to you, but now it's time to give birth to yourself! Whether or not you are adopted or abandoned or in a loving family, your mother still gave birth to you. Prior to that, your mother and father conceived you. These are truly baby steps. They sewed the genetic seed for who you are and, hopefully, your mother, father, grandparents, foster parents or adoptive parents taught you to walk, talk and understand the world.

Thereafter, no one said, "now it's time to give birth to yourself." Who you are, has instead been shaped and guided and managed and nagged and formed to conform. In fact, even parents with the best intentions want their children to be safe, happy and to do well in the world, so they enrol you in classes and get you to work hard and try to make sure you do well in school, and, when you answer back or don't cooperate, you are disciplined. This is necessary to help you become your best self, and yet sometimes it can mean you dilute yourself to fit in at home and fit in to what society wants from you.

So, when I say 'give birth to yourself', I mean it's time for the rebirth of the *true you* - who you truly are.

That is YOU - who you are. Yes you may have traits of your mother and father and ancestors; you may have even been given the name of some of your nearest and dearest, but you are not them. This is what we have been investigating in this book.

Giving birth to yourself is finding out what floats your boat and sailing where you want to go - not staying in the boat that you were born in and believing the wind will never change.

Now is your time to take responsibility and turn the sail and steer the boat in the direction you want to sail in. Hopefully people will wish you "bon voyage" but, if they don't, it may say more about their fears than yours.

You're in the process of lifting the anchor that was keeping you weighed down and stuck. Once you are set free, you can sail towards your dream life.

That's why, in this chapter we'll explore:

- How to uncover what floats your boat, and what your chosen destination and journey looks like in real terms?

- How do you want your story to pan out? You hold the pen now, so you get to write it.

- How to figure out who to keep on board (who is sailing with you and who isn't)?

- How to use all of your life experiences, good and bad, as fuel to steer you in the right direction?

- Why forgiving the past and focusing on the present enables you to point your boat forward towards a hopeful and meaningful future?

Whether we use a sailing boat or a storybook analogy, the point of this chapter is about regaining control; taking responsibility for your own life, your own story, your own journey.

You are the author and the central protagonist. You are the captain of your ship. And, at the end of the day, everything you desire - perhaps it's a nice house, holiday, healthy family members, a job you enjoy - none of them can bring joy if the receiver of these desires (you) is not tuned in to joy.

It's a bit like having the best television or computer but without a wi-fi system. A television aerial without a receiver is no use.

So you are the receiver and the receiver has to be in good working order, which means happiness comes from within. You need to be ready and able to receive joy. This means, there needs to be space available for happiness to come from within. If 'within' is full of repressed rubbish, that is not feeding your spirit, because it has come from someone else's choice.

Once and for all - we are done with letting other people choose for us!

We are giving birth to ourselves.

We are writing our own story.

We are steering our own boat.

Remember, it is not your fault what happened to you. Any experience you've been through, or the fact that other directors have been writing your story up until this point. It's how the world around us shapes us, it's a natural phenomenon, so that's not your fault. Just as it's not their fault, the ones who've conditioned you. Because they've endured the same conditioning. Realising this leads to forgiveness, which we'll cover later in the chapter.

However, if you choose not to fight for your freedom now that you know the truth, you will likely blame yourself for that. And I don't want that for you. You owe it to yourself to fight for your freedom, otherwise you do to yourself what they did to you. You suppress yourself and hand the pen back to them.

And, when it comes to that television or computer system - if we're going ensure we can receive, we need to make sure the programmes we receive are the ones we want to watch; we need to have the remote in our own hands. Living life where your thoughts and beliefs are conditioned by others is like watching the TV but handing the remote control over to someone else, permanently. And we all know how frustrating sitting through the umpteenth episode of someone else's preferred viewing can be!

Until now, we've had this super television, but someone else has chosen the programmes we watch.

But we're not doing that anymore!

Not only because, in letting others have the remote we relinquish control over what we watch, but because what we want to watch changes over time.

As we grow in life our tastes change. When we were small we may have loved all the children's programmes, when we were teenagers we may have loved Top of the Pops. As we grow a little older we may enjoy documentaries or certain types of films.

Life is always change. In fact, the only constant we can be certain of is change itself. The seasons change, the wind changes, the tide changes, the weather changes, so why wouldn't we? Change is growth. If we are not changing, then we become stagnant and, for most people, that is when the rot the disappointment and fed up feelings take root.

We became a chameleon of sorts (false self) be it the sensible one, the daring one, the entertainer, the drinker, the over eater and, when it doesn't do anything for us anymore to assume that role, we have lost our fix and don't want to do it anymore.

The definition of insanity is to keep doing the same and expect different results. So in order to grow and change and be reborn into our true selves, the self that we owe ourselves to be, we need to do things differently, we need to make some changes. And, when we do that, we can break free.

This chapter will give you the final key to unlock your future potential. In fact, it'll do more than that; it'll enable you to be your own key cutter. No, better still, it will let you be the designer of your own lock, designer of your own home (the truest version of yourself) and designer of your own life!

Put it this way, if you had all the money in the world, would you buy a house where the entire design and colour scheme and choice of bedding and ornaments had been chosen by someone else? What if you bought the perfect house in the perfect location and it was all decorated in pink, but you don't like pink - would you keep it pink or redecorate to your own taste?

Well, once you have completed the exercises in this chapter, uncovered your own value and desires and given birth to your truest you, you'll be able to make your own choice.

When you have the skill of the locksmith, you are never locked out. All this time you've been using someone else's key to your own lock, but now you can use your own key, design your own lock and you can even help others if they are locked out.

However, if someone attempts to use their key on you it will no longer fit meaning that you will be able to discern straight away which ideas do not belong to you.

This is not to say that you should tell someone else they are wrong and impose your ideas on to them. Rather, in respecting them you are respecting yourself. And this means you have finally reached the optimum state - you are in balance.

Once you have achieved balance you have achieved FREEDOM, peace and joy. You will be able to live in the present moment, because you know you can protect and balance yourself and have response-ability.

And, best of all, you are able to add the F into the LIE to create your own wonderful LIFE.

Stopping the LIE to put the F back into LIFE

To summarise, you now know that you first were led to live a lie as it was based on someone else's ideas and values and choices and you anaesthetised your feelings in order to fit in, belong and conform. Depression, anxiety or OCD perhaps then showed up to let you know you were off track, that your roller coaster ride was veering off course. You then had to emote the fact that you were not happy and investigate some of the why not's and to let yourself FEEL your way again, to get the sat nav back on course. You've had to understand that the guilt of not pleasing people is a crazy idea for all parties. You've had to learn to express not repress with love at all times to remain free and true to yourself to get your life back.

Throughout this book, we've been thinking about the F in our lives so we can stop the LIE and start living a LIFE. We've explored the importance of Feelings, Fear, Forgiveness, and Freedom.

You now have the knowledge and the tools. But in this chapter, you'll learn the final jigsaw piece of the puzzle - and be fully equipped with the tools you need to live the life you've dreamed of.

In this chapter we'll put more Fs back into the LIE to create your LIFE, so you can:

- Forgive The Past
- Focus on The Present
- Look Forward
- Go with the Flow
- Find Your Thrive Tribe

It's time to replace comparison and competition and judgement with curiosity, gratitude and an ability to honour your emotions and feel your feelings and be ok with that.

Remember, change is growth and, in reading this book, you've been given a second chance to live YOUR life YOUR way, as YOURSELF.

So, let's get started...

Fail. It's useful! Because, everything counts!

It's time to learn once and for all that every experience you go through provides you with the fuel you need to steer your boat in the right direction.

Please grab a pen and a piece of paper and jot down every time you can remember failing or making a mistake. Just free-write without giving much thought for no longer than a minute or two.

This might make you feel sad or annoyed or disappointed at first. It will likely make you critical about yourself, which is human nature. We do that. It's something we do as a survival mechanism to try to make ourselves better. And yet, what we ALL OFTEN FAIL AT is reminding ourselves that we are good enough. What's more, research has shown that self-criticism doesn't motivate us to improve; it just makes us feel bad about ourselves. So if we really want to improve, we're better off looking for the bright spots; noticing what we're doing well and succeeding at, rather than focusing on everything we've done wrong.

Why am I asking you to write down everything you've done wrong then? You may ask. Well, because I want you to find the value in those mistakes and failures.

The good, the bad and the ugly - it's all data

So that's your next task. Please jot down the lesson or value or data from experiencing those difficulties, from making those mistakes. If you struggle with this, read the next few paragraphs first for some examples and then proceed. But please make sure you do this part of the exercise as it's important you do.

For example, it could be that you made a mistake entering in to a relationship with someone (even though you didn't know then what you know now, so give yourself a break there). But actually, that relationship may well have taught you exactly what you DON'T want from a relationship. You may have made a mistake trusting someone untrustworthy, but perhaps the pain you've experienced as a result taught you that you're stronger than you thought you were? You may ruminate about how you weren't there for someone who needed you but, perhaps the guilt you've felt about that has reminded you to be there for others ever since. Even if the lesson isn't obvious, there's data in every experience we endure.

That's why, if you take one message from this book, I hope you are able to remind yourself often that EVERYTHING COUNTS towards your growth, even the difficult and uncomfortable experiences you've faced and may face again; especially the difficult and uncomfortable experiences. In fact - that's where we learn the most about ourselves - our true selves - amid the muck and chaos and hardships, and so that data is particularly useful.

Everything you go through and have ever gone through is useful to teach you about yourself, and knowing yourself is so important. It's why I've written this book, to help you go from LIE to LIFE. Indeed, the more you know yourself, the more self-awareness you have, the better able you are to have self-compassion. And living life with self-compassion is a warmer place to be.

Not only that, the more you know about yourself, the more you know what matters most to you - so the better you become at uncovering your happiness value - and the more you can make choices in your daily life to spend the minutes of your days doing what matters most with those who matters most and nourishing the person who matters most of all in living your best life - YOU!

This is why it's so important to take responsibility for your own choices and decisions, even if you end up making massive mistakes or failing.

For that reason, I'd like to get rid of the term 'failing miserably' and replace it with 'failing joyfully'. As we discussed in Chapter 7 - failure is more useful than success. But we tend to veer away from taking responsibility for our failures.

Yet responsibility is the key to freedom.

Response-ability is your responsibility

Responsibility can sound like something we don't want, because, responsibility means the buck stops with us. When we spend our life giving up our own ideals and values to someone else, letting others direct our story, we may fool ourselves in staying in that place by saying, 'well at least I can blame them if things don't work out'.

This is one of the reasons why we continue to hand over control of our story to external directors. It can feel easier when we feel like giving up. We can just blame them and let them shoulder responsibility.

But hold on!!! This is YOUR life. Why would you want to do anything other than try to make the most of it - to at least try? When you do not shoulder responsibility, you give up trying.

The blame game can seem like a get out clause from failing or feeling like we've got it wrong, but it's also a get out clause for LIVING! When you give control and responsibility for your life to someone else, you are not living your life, you are living a lie. You don't want that. How do I know that you don't want that?

Because you are reading this book! You are wanting to put the F back into that LIE, so you can live your LIFE!

Sometimes, the fear of feeling like we've got it wrong is the main reason we relinquish control, which is why removing our fear of failure is so important.

So what if we fail or get it wrong? We're only human. Everyone makes mistakes. And, as we know - mistakes are the most useful learning tools we have. They give us more data than doing everything right does.

And, frankly, anyone who wants to point out that you got it wrong are not busy enough getting it right for themselves. People who are ready to point out that you failed are often frightened you are going to succeed, because they dare not have a go themselves. People who point out your failures are often scared of even trying (and jealous that you have done so) and your failure simply feeds their resolve to stay where they are - stagnant.

You cannot grow without some failure. So please do not avoid living your life!

Have the ability to respond to what life gives you and take responsibility for your own life.

Fail sometimes and laugh. Successful people have failed and learned a lot from their failings. If the baby never tried again to walk because he failed we would all still be crawling. Don't crawl through your life. Stand tall and walk the talk.

Forget the people who are watching for your failings. What people think of us is none of our business. And besides, they're too busy worrying what we think of them! The irony of caring too much about what others might think.

So Response-Ability is the way to go. Once our SatNav (our feelings) start to guide us, let's RESPOND, let's feel the feelings, no matter what they are, and find the ability to achieve our own dreams.

Change means we are responsible for our lives, we are no longer giving the control to someone else. No more repression, no more fear, no more anxiety, just living joyfully the way we want to live.

Now, I'd like you to write down the following:

I am responsible for my own life from now on.
My mistakes, bad decisions, failures are USEFUL.
They equip me with knowledge, about myself, about what

matters most, about how not to do things. But they are helpful to me.

Then I want you to write a heading called '**Bright Parts**'. I want you to get curious about what you do well or what you do right. You might struggle at first because your negative bias conditioning - something we all have - focuses on what you do wrong (although remember it's never wrong because it all counts, it's data). But just practice using this noticing muscle over the next few weeks and noticing the things you don't do badly, the things you're ok at, even good at. Then write them down.

You are more likely to be able to make the changes you want in your life when you focus on the good. Because nobody likes being criticised, even when it's by yourself. The proven science shows that people are more likely to make long-lasting positive changes when they notice what they're doing well and then, when you notice areas that may need improvement (more sleep, more exercise, and so on) you can notice those with less judgement and take tiny steps towards improving them.

Find your forte and shine like the diamond you are

I'd like you now to spend 20 minutes doing a test - it's a test which will show you what your character strengths are - http://www.viacharacter.org/

These strengths may have been buried for a long time, or they may be noticeable. Either way, this is an incredibly accurate test created and used by positive psychology scientists. Once you know your top five character strengths, you can start to use them in your day to day life. We now know that the more you use your character strengths in your life, the higher your level of life-satisfaction and well-being. It makes sense. Far better to uncover what makes you shine and use it, rather than to focus on what makes you suffer.

With that in mind, I have a question for you:

What is a diamond?

A jewel you may say, a precious jewel and yes, you are right.

But, to become a diamond, it started as a piece of coal that stuck to its job.

It lived underground and was pushed and rubbed and then it shone.

This is what we have to do with ourselves, we have to find our shine and sparkle.

If we don't, we remain that piece of carbon waiting for someone else to notice that we have a talent.

We have to find our own genius like the greats.

Uncovering your character strengths is the first part of that.

I cannot believe that only a handful of us have genius. Apparently Edison who invented the light bulb said his 999 failed attempts taught him how not to do it. He never stopped believing; he kept going and he found the light literally.

Don't we all love the story of someone who was told they can't do something, so they go away and prove that yes, they can. JK Rowling's Harry Potter manuscript was rejected multiple times, but she never gave up.

Do not give up. Become like that piece of coal, use your depression and your anxiety to shine.

Here's how:

Revisit your notes about all the stuff that you feel you've done wrong and add to that any other adversities or hardships that may have been out of your control and not your fault at all.

Write it all down.

Now I want you to thank it all.

Thank all the shit that helped you to grow!

Even thank your depression, anxiety or OCD and other ailments, because they showed up to protect you - they provided you with an early warning signal that the roller coaster cart was veering off track, your ship was steering away from your TRUE ROUTE and was misaligned with what you truly want and who you truly are. So it's given you helpful data about yourself and your life and your relationships; about what you don't like or want. Now you can use that data like a scientist to uncover what you do like and want. You can uncover what truly matters to you and you can start to build a life by putting the F back into it - via Forgiveness, Flow, and the Freedom of Feeling.

The next thing we have to do is FORGIVE the past.

Forgive the past and get the key to unlock your future

The more you know about yourself and how you want the story of your life to be, the easier it is to unlock your potential (with the skill of the locksmith) and break free from the past towards the freedom of your future.

The other way to break free from the past is to release it. And the best way to do that is to forgive.

Of course, when we begin to feel our way back to life and realise one of the reasons we haven't been feeling our best is because our true self has been repressed, it is quite normal to feel angry or hurt about having been conditioned or hypnotised with someone else's ideas or values.

Personally, I think it's worth permitting yourself to feel those repressed feelings of anger at first; to allow yourself your terrible two tantrum even if you are 40. As you now know, feeling your emotions is how to release and express them. But try not to hold on to them for too long, as wallowing in them after you've expressed those feelings can be toxic to you and can cause psychosomatic symptoms at best and sometimes chronic illness.

Once we've felt those feelings and made the conscious choice to express rather than repress them, we can begin the forgiveness process.

Once you start to see things from this true perspective of repression and how hurt people hurt people regarding the trans-generational hot potato, **forgiveness** is possible.

Asking yourself to forgive someone when you are still taking it personally is almost impossible. It is not true forgiveness if it will still be repressed and trouble you and hold you back. So it's worth really working hard to forgive.

Once you understand fully then you hopefully feel different towards that person and are able to say to yourself, "Forgive them for they know not what they do." Sometimes you still may choose not to have a relationship with that person, and that's ok, but it's important that you no longer carry any toxic thoughts for them or within yourself.

Obviously if you have really been abused in a way that is very difficult for you then please reach out for professional help.

Being force fed values that you now realise weren't for you feels as awful as being fed food that is not to your taste. If you had the latter you would probably be ill. So feeling emotionally and mentally ill is an understandable process when we put it in that context. When, after being force fed, you are physically sick, you'd reject that food and stand up to the 'feeder' and refuse the food. It's the same with being force fed values. You don't have to physically go and stand up to your parents or society or whoever has led to you anaesthetising your true feelings and steering away from your true values and true calling. But you can make a stand by saying to yourself. 'That's enough. I'm in control now.'

Try it. Go and stand in front of the mirror and say, 'That's enough, I'm in control now'.

Then say, 'I forgive you' - you are saying this to your repressors.

Now write this down in your notebook. Write down:

I am in control now.

I forgive you. Then write who you forgive and what you forgive them for.

Once you have released the past and forgiven people, try not to keep administering it to yourself again and again. Your aim is to get better not bitter, so let the past go.

Depression is repression usually from the past carried as a model for relating to others.

Anxiety is usually about a future event where you may give up your position

Obsessive compulsive thinking is usually born out of not having control and over thinking every eventuality.

Repressed anger plays a big part in all these conditions. We don't have to blow a fuse, we can become like the pressure cooker and release with love.

The past is behind you and you're not going that way. You can't do anything about the past, it's already happened, it's done, it's over. So forgive and move on.

Once you've released the past, once you've let it go, there are only two possible areas on which to focus - the present and the future.

Often when people are anxious it is usually about the future - about what might happen. OCD is an extreme of this when you try to gain some control over things. But we already know that over-thinking and pre-empting worst case scenarios doesn't stop future events from happening, it only spoils the present moment.

In Chapter 6, we looked at how to get your anxious thoughts back into perspective, to protect worries about future 'what ifs' from spiralling out of control. Revisit that chapter if you need to, because the only way I want you to view the future is with HOPE!

Once you've released the past, the next step is to focus on the present, because only when we tune in to today and get into the flow of RIGHT NOW, can we figure out what matters most to us. This process leads us to feel more hopeful about our future.

Focus on the present to figure out what matters most

There are many books written about peace and contentment, about being able to live in the now, in the present moment. Yet, if the past is still taking you hostage then it can be difficult to focus on your now and to find that inner-peace.

I love all the books available on living in the now. Eckhart Tolle is my favourite. I love mindfulness and books on miracles and I believe them all. However, until you are free from the past it may be impossible for you to get yourself back into that all important present moment.

As is our way, if you struggle with it, you may start to tell yourself that you're a lost cause, and that is NEVER true. Mindfulness and focusing on the present moment takes practice. But before you practice focusing on the present, you need to use the power within you to release the past, so that you can experience the power of 'nowness' and unlock your potential in the future. Please use that power.

Return to now

The people who write about living in the now and being present have found it! They too were once the same as you and now they are free. I want the same for you, so let's remove the blocks right away.

This exercise will help bring you back to 'now', to your present.

First, slowly, take a big deep breath in for the count of four, hold for four and breathe out for five.

Now, focus on what you can see around you - use your sense of sight and say to yourself what you can see right now.

For example, 'I can see my computer keyboard, the light switch, the window and the door handle.'

Next focus on what you can hear - use your sense of hearing and say to yourself what you can hear right now.

For example, 'I can hear someone mowing their lawn, the birds tweeting outside the window and my tummy rumbling.'

Repeat this exercise with what you can smell, taste and touch.

For this period of time you were likely caught up in the process of noticing what your senses could feel and, as a result, were focusing on the present moment - on what you could see, hear, feel, taste and touch right now.

That's a quick and easy way to ground yourself to the present.

Another way is to focus on your breath and, each time you notice your mind wandering, as it absolutely will do - guaranteed, you just simply bring your attention back to your breath and watch the thought float away like a cloud. And each time your mind wanders, there's no need to judge or get frustrated, simply say 'in' and 'out' and bring your focus back to your breath, each time. That is the basis of mindfulness.

"If you just sit and observe, you will see how restless your mind is... but, over time it does calm, and... you start to see things more clearly,"
Steve Jobs

By using these exercises regularly, you'll find yourself dwelling on your past less and worrying about your future less, because, when you get fully present, you become free.

Of course, this is not to say you will never be judgemental about what you've said or done or had said or done to you in the past, nor that you will never ever worry about what might happen in the future again. You're human after all and we are wired to be cautious and judgemental as part of our inner survival mechanism. But, you will be able to bring yourself back to the present more often, to reframe inaccurate judgemental thoughts and gain perspective if worries look like they might spiral, as we've learned in previous chapters.

And you'll be able to bring yourself back to now with these exercises whenever you want. Because, now that we're recovering from other people's control, rather than pick up from where they left off, we can live life in the moment and see where life takes us from there.

In fact, if we immerse ourselves in life more, in what is happening right now, from moment to moment, we won't be immersed in our repression, we'll instead observe and notice what makes us feel good, what makes us feel bad and build up a clearer picture of the things we do want and don't want in our lives in the future.

If we start living more spontaneously and more in the present moment perhaps the banquet is lying there right in front of us. Up until now we've been too busy wearing our convoluted spectacles, that we couldn't see a thing. But now we can approach life with our eyes wide open and be better able to see what matters most to us.

Opening our eyes in this way also leads to greater self-acceptance. Because, when you find balance you'll be better able to appreciate your life and yourself 'warts and all' - as you are. You've cleaned the lens and are now better able to see that you are already good enough.

The other benefit of living in the present moment and being able to see more clearly what matters to you, is you are then better able to focus on those things, feelings, people, relationships. This is wonderful because, as the law of attraction tells us, what we focus on, we attract.

Up until now, if you've experienced depression or anxiety, you'll have focused a lot of your mental energy and thoughts on past regrets and future worries and current judgements and may have inadvertently attracted more of what you don't want into your life. Now you have an incredible opportunity - to attract what you DO WANT into your life.

Our minds can't help but focus on what we think about because we have an 'attention bias'. If I tell you - 'don't think about pink elephants,' what are you now thinking about? All your mind will focus on is pink elephants. That's why we can't tell ourselves to 'stop thinking about something negative'. The only way we can change negative thoughts is to hear them and then replace them through reframing and gaining perspective, as learned in Chapter 6.

However, the same is true with positive thoughts. We want to focus on them, and we have the power to do so.

So focus on what you are grateful to have NOW in the present moment and focus on what you want to have in the FUTURE and this is what your mind will focus on.

Exercise

I want you to devote time each day for the next seven days to focus on what you are grateful to have NOW in your life. Write down what you are grateful for. Feel how you feel after doing this exercise. I always find it makes me feel better and scientists have discovered that feeling appreciative, writing down three things we're grateful for as often as we can and writing thank you letters to ourselves and to others has such a positive impact on our well-being that six months after we start this practice, we are still feeling WAY better than before we started.

Forward - look forward not back

Just as it's important for our mental health to focus our attention on the present, it's also important to look forward and dream about the kind of future we desire, rather than look back at the past. It's time to dream.

Freedom is ours to choose, if we wallow in the past and keep the old repressed stuff, like filling an attic, then there is no way we have the energy to clear out and we will stay in the prison of our very own making. Instead, by forgiving and moving forward, we are having a mental de-clutter and we are free of all the junk we've collected over the years.

We are finding the key here, you always had it. Discovering it can be elating.

Once we've de-cluttered, we get to choose what we fill our minds with and there is nothing wrong with filling it with hopes and dreams, because that means we are looking forward. We can book things in the diary that we can look forward to (not things that make us anxious, only things that we feel comfortable about doing, with people who lift us up - more on focusing our attention on those people at the end of this chapter). But, not only can we book activities which excite and energise us, we can also spend time on our hopes, those things which bring a sense of meaning to our lives.

Finding meaning

Prisoners of war dreamed of their freedom day. Those who survived often spoke of the wonderful things they were going to do when they were released. According to Victor Frankl in his book, *Man's Search For Meaning*, this dream kept them alive as they held hope for the future (which even gave their current life meaning). They may have been languishing in concentration camps but, this hope for the future kept them going, as opposed to those who gave up hope, who lost the will to live and died.

Interestingly when the war ended and the doors opened a lot of them just sat for a while as they had become institutionalised of course. Their prison was their safety and their dream didn't have to become real, they didn't have to be responsible for it but it provided hope.

And that was the key ingredient to spur them on.

Hope and the dream are the ingredients that can provide the fuel for driving this dream and hope into life.

When we spend all of our time looking back rather than forward, we make our own prison. Don't make your own prison. Freedom is yours for the taking.

Let's give life to our dreams. Your dreams are your life. You may be like the best timber to light the best fire that gives the most warmth but, if you have nothing to light it with, the fire dies. Don't let your best dream, or idea die a death. See it spark there and add another log to the fire each time you think about it.

Because freedom from the past means freedom for the future - your future. By going through each of the chapters in this book, you are gradually putting the F back into what was once a LIE. You give an F about your LIFE, and now you're putting the F back into it.

You are starting to save up with your dreams. You are depositing into an account which has your name on it. Each time you dream with hope for the future, you deposit your richness and your individuality and you feel what you are saving for. In this way you now have the ability to respond to what happens in your life out of those lenses. You now have 20/20 vision and are in, or on the journey towards, psychological health. A good position to be in.

Now it's time for the final puzzle piece - to set intentions for your future; to find out what really floats your boat. So grab a pen to rewrite your story and become the author of your dream life.

The final puzzle piece

Please write in your notepad your answers to the following questions. I'd like you to do this exercise twice.

Once without much thought - just free-writing and letting whatever flows out of your pen flow out of your pen.

The second time you can go back and add to your list, with a little more thought. In fact, the second time I'd like you to really visualise it and try to FEEL it; to see yourself in your mind's eye living that life - really see it. Think about what you can see, hear, taste, touch and smell when you get to the question about your dream life. And don't let any judgements or barriers get in the way.

First, get present and take some deep slow breaths in and out and focus on your senses. Then go through each question one-by-one.

What do you want?

What do you want to spend your time doing?

What matters most to you?

Who matters most to you?

Why?

If money/time was no object - What does your dream life look like?

In one year from now what are you doing?

In five years from now what are you doing?

I want you to visualise your answers to these questions as often as you can. Perhaps every night before you go to sleep - picture, in your mind's eye - all that you hope for. Don't dismiss it as impossible, just allow yourself to dream... and just hope.

Next, think about three tiny actions you could take to help bring your dreams to fruition. You may have dreamed of living in the middle of a forest. So plan to go on a 15 minute woodland walk each day. You may have dreamed of becoming a chef. Perhaps you could enrol in an evening class or watch a cooking video on YouTube every night this week. Action is where you get traction. Remember, these actions can be tiny. Just five minutes of dancing round your kitchen can lead you to a more habitual exercise practice. When you get real about your hopes for the future you can make space in your mind for small activities you can bring in to your daily life which could help make your dreams a reality. By making them small, you are more likely to do them. And that may spark you towards taking another action and another, baby steps towards creating your dream life.

Once you've done that, it's time to remind yourself to go with the flow.

Go with the flow

IMPORTANT NOTE - remember, like John Lennon said, often life happens to you while you are busy making plans. So often your dreams won't materialise in the way you hope or imagine them to.

Sometimes things can get worse before they get better - you get a parking ticket and an expensive trip to the dentist before landing your dream job, for instance. It often takes longer than you'd hoped to find a home or holiday or relationship that you'd longed for. But you'll still get there; you'll still achieve your dreams. Why? Because you took the first tiny step towards it by getting clear on what you want from life and doing something, anything, to start to make it happen, no matter how small.

So bearing that in mind, it's important that, once we've set our intentions, we then embrace the flow of life.

This reminds me of a quote from John O'Donohue:

"I would love to live Like a river flows, Carried by the surprise of its own unfolding."

So go with the flow. In assuming control over others opinions and taking responsibility, it's important that we learn to loosen the leash and let things flow as they do.

That's where balance comes in again. Now that you've regained control over your thoughts and values and feelings you may not feel like letting go, but I'm not suggesting you let go entirely, just that you maintain control over what you think, feel and do (i.e. how you respond) but that you let go of how your dreams manifest.

This is the ultimate way to live, trusting that everything will align in time and work out, even if it takes longer than you'd hoped. Acceptance is as important as balance here.

So accept that along the way there will still be ups and downs (because life is a rollercoaster) and things won't always go to plan, because now you are better equipped to cope when things go off track, because you know they'll get back on track soon enough, now that you're in the driving seat, now that you are better able to re-frame thoughts that don't serve you, surround yourself with people who uplift you rather than put you down and now that you are able to see through clear lenses.

So embrace the ride. Focus on your dream life, but know that the way it will happen might not be the way you think it will. Accept that it may be a long winding road and you may think you are lost, but when you get there and reflect back, all the dots will join up.

Even the lost times, the disappointing times, it will all make sense if you just keep the belief. And remember, even those times count. It's all data!

I guess that is what belief is - it is faith that you will get there even when the signs say different.

I guess then you could call that a miracle - something that happens when it looks like it won't.

When you have hope for the future, anything is possible. And that's a beautiful feeling.

Now that you've

- Forgiven The Past

- Focused on The Present

- Looked Forward

- Gone with the Flow

It's time to remember that you are not alone. As human beings we're in this together. There are many people who've been through what you have and there are people who want you to thrive. Even just one person is enough. So now, it's time to consider who you're inviting on board onto the boat you're steering, to:

- Find Your Thrive Tribe

During this process, you may find some people don't fit in your life or, maybe they don't want to be, and that's ok. They may feel anxious or jealous about this new you. Please do not feel guilty about the fact you did not remain serving those people at the expense of your own happiness.

This is YOUR life.

Other people in your life are likely to still be viewing their life and yours through convoluted spectacles. Celebrate that you did not collude with them because, if we serve people and end up repressed or depressed and do not express it to them, then we also rob them of a chance to re-think.

Your changes may inspire them to change too.

And when we change, we grow.

Of course, be open to compromise, but ensure that your relationships are balanced - that there is give and take, that there is integrity and authenticity for a healthy relationship based on trust and goodwill.

Many depressed people are empaths. When our childhood programming has been to avoid upsetting mum or dad, then the child is so acutely aware of other peoples' moods. As a result, they tune in and soak up other people's anxiety or depression like a sponge.

Often depressed people have spent so much time soaking up other people's feelings that they are carrying someone else's pain and, what's worse, they are still identifying with it as their own.

When these people recover from their own depression often they can make brilliant therapists, nurses, and healers of all kinds. To avoid burnout though, these people have to learn to protect themselves from absorbing other peoples repressed feelings.

Let us just remind ourselves that some individuals are still not aware that they have numbed their feelings, or they believe they live quite well without acknowledging their own or anyone else's, they still have the belief that feeling is not necessary.

Often a person who does feel or cry can then start to believe the non-feeling person has more control. Control is the operative word because they are not in touch with their feelings and may berate someone for NOT controlling theirs (the keep calm and carry on regime). We have investigated at length that repressing or ignoring your feelings can lead to depression, anxiety, over drinking, OCD and more, and we don't want the coping strategies, we want freedom.

So we can't force other people to feel their repressed feelings, but we have to honour ours for our freedom, so we don't revert to conforming. Remember soft and strong is the way forward, Expression not Repression.

So if you come across someone who would prefer you not to express your feelings and has no empathy for your expression, be careful not to start to feel guilty because you have angered or upset them.

Some people in our world will never be wrong and never accept your feelings, these people are called narcissistic and often find a willing over sensitive person (empath) to project their criticism onto.

Trans-generationally they (the narcissist) have probably been around others who did not respond or model how to do feelings or conversely been so pandered to that the narcissistic person has not learned to have empathy for the other and expects to be right all the time.

As such, we can forgive these people. But we can also gain control back by knowing when to keep them at a distance.

Learning to discern what is happening becomes much easier once we are more sure of ourselves and trust ourselves more.

As you focus more on the present and have more hope for the future, as you start to express your feelings rather than repress them, and as you free yourself from the shackles of the past, you'll begin to notice more quickly which people suit your own energy and trust your own instincts around who to keep close and who to keep at arm's reach.

Finding your thrive tribe because other people matter

Have you ever spent time with someone who makes you feel drained? Or who make you feel bad about yourself? Can you notice the difference when you have you spent time with people who lift your spirit and even if you have been feeling low, they help you to feel vibrant again?

While it's crucial for your future good health to ensure that YOU stay in the driving seat of your own life and ensure that other people's thoughts and beliefs do not write your story, it's important to have a sense of belonging and to be able to trust at least one person. Supportive relationships are a major pillar of well-being, as positive psychology scientists have found.

Belonging is a basic human need. So think about who in your life wants you to thrive? If you can't think of anyone, it's ok, there will be people you'll feel a deep connection with who can enter your life now that you have cleared away the junk. And now that you have a closer connection to your gut instinct, you'll know who to trust.

The good news about being your own casting director is - you get to choose WHO joins you in your story; who to invite on the journey.

Now you have the freedom to be yourself, believe in yourself and achieve what you want. Hope and meaning create freedom in the future. And, now that you are FREE, you can bring hope and meaning into your life.

What's more, by uncovering what matters most and taking steps toward doing more of what you love, you can find and turn the key in the lock.

Congratulations - you are now free! Enjoy your freedom. Enjoy living the life you deserve - now that you have put the F into what was once a LIE - you are free to go and live your LIFE!

What a wonderful journey you have ahead.